Spoils
of
War

SPOILS OF WAR

A Play by
Michael Weller

Garden City, New York

For Rosa

SPOILS OF WAR was commissioned by and had its world premiere at The Second Stage, artistic directors Carole Rothman and Robyn Goodman. The first cast was as follows:

Martin . . . . Christopher Collet
Andrew . . . . Larry Bryggman
Elise . . . . Kate Nelligan
Penny . . . . Annette Bening
Emma . . . . Alice Playten
Lew . . . . Kevin O'Rourke

(The playwright would like to credit these three actors whose roles were cut from the play prior to its premiere: James Rebhorn as the older Martin, Cheryl Giannini as his wife Celia and Anthony Picciano as Morty, a Party Guest.)

A rewritten version of the play ran at Toronto's Royal Alexandra Theatre and then moved to the Music Box Theatre, opening on Broadway on November 10, 1988. It was produced, in association with The Second Stage, by Ed and David Mirvish. Austin Pendleton directed, as he had the earlier productions. Scenery was designed by Andrew Jackness; costumes by Ruth Morley; lighting by Paul Gallo; and sound by Gary and Timmy Harris. The cast was as follows:

Martin . . . . Christopher Collet
Andrew . . . . Jeffrey DeMunn
Elise . . . . Kate Nelligan
Penny . . . . Marita Geraghty
Emma . . . . Alice Playten
Lew . . . . Kevin O'Rourke

The author would like to thank American Express, which through the Fund for New American Plays program gave him money to write this play.

CHARACTERS

MARTIN, the son, age 16
ANDREW, his father, early 40s
ELISE, his mother, early 40s
PENNY, father's girlfriend, 20s
EMMA, mother's friend, late 30s
LEW, a builder, 20s

TIME

The 1950s

PLACE

New York City

ACT
ONE

ACT ONE

(ELISE's *place, a cramped apartment on the fifth floor of a dingy Greenwich Village walkup.*

MARTIN *comes into the doorway, holding a valise. He surveys the room: unmade pullout sofa bed with ash tray on it, heaped with cigarette butts; half-read books on side table. The only visible storage is a crudely made wall-length affair with rod for hanging clothes and a bureau at one end inside. A curtain, now open, runs its length when closed, concealing the clutter within. Across the window, in matching material, is a curtain pulled shut. When it is open, we can see part of a neon sign that runs vertically outside, showing the letters H–A–R and the top of an M [for "Pharmacy"].*

It is the mid–1950s.

MARTIN *enters, sets down the valise and begins straightening up, folding bed away, etc. He is just sixteen, his face still boyish and open, but with a veiled, secretive quality which shows itself from time to time. He rarely looks people in the eye. Noting the darkness of the room, he approaches the window to pull open the curtains. As he does so,* ELISE *enters and the room fills with light.* MARTIN *turns and sees her.)*

MARTIN: Mom!

ELISE: Angel!

(ELISE, *breathless, sets down sketch case and shopping bag full of magazines.)*

ELISE: Sorry I'm late, they put us on double overtime again, have you been here long, God my feet are killing me, those stairs, let me look at you! Just as I thought, the handsomest man in the universe. Welcome home, angel!

(As they embrace, what sounds like Mexican bullfight music begins to play from next door, festive and bright. ELISE *is in her early forties, with a gypsy-like beauty and a playful, seductive manner that is unconscious and natural. But there are also a poise and reserve about her that suggest a person who has learned to put a brave face on her loneliness. She is dressed for a wilting hot day in the early summer, something handmade that, like all her clothing, shows her own unique sense of flair and style. At their embrace, the music swells from next door.)*

ELISE: Now then, first things first—how was the train ride down?

MARTIN: Just a train ride. Why is it so hot in here?

ELISE: It's nearly summer, that's why: Cold in winter, hot in summer, any complaints see the man in the moon.

(Through the following, ELISE *sits, removes shoes, massages feet, checks frayed hem, then pulls magazines from shopping bag and sorts them into piles on the table.)*

MARTIN: I'll open the window.

ELISE: The noise will drown out Mrs. Salvatore's music. She put her speakers right up against the wall especially for me, lovely neighbor, a gypsy, like your mother.

MARTIN: I'll turn on the fan . . .

ELISE: Stupid thing, two days after I had it repaired, *kaput,* a waste of money. Speaking of which, I'm the tiniest bit short till payday, so a major decision has to be made about this evening—dinner or a movie, you choose.

MARTIN: I'm seeing some friends from school.

ELISE: On your first night home?

MARTIN: It was kind of last minute, on the train ride.

ELISE: What am I running here, a halfway house for transient teens?

MARTIN: My summer job doesn't start till next Monday and there's an early train upstate, we have the whole week together . . . (MARTIN *exits with his suitcase)*

ELISE: May I then expect the pleasure of his company on his last, if not his first night home?

MARTIN: *(reenters)* Absolutely.

ELISE: Sunday night, make a note.

MARTIN: *(smiles)* "Note."

ELISE: Now tell me all about Parent's Day. Did you read your essay out loud? In front of the entire school? Did they applaud, and anyone who didn't their name and address, I'll deal with them personally.

MARTIN: It went fine, Mom.

ELISE: "It went fine, Mom." Now doesn't that conjure a vivid picture, yes, I see it all . . .

MARTIN: I'll tell you while we eat, okay?

ELISE: Excellent! Raid the icebox, whatever you find, that's dinner. *(Plops down some magazines conspicuously)*

MARTIN: Why the magazines?

ELISE: *(reads titles) Construction Quarterly—Contractor's Annual—Perspectives in Extruded Plastic.* These titles are sheer poetry.

MARTIN: *(on the way out)* Changing careers again? *(exits)*

ELISE: Don't be such a Smart Smerdley, your mother has had the inspiration of a lifetime.

MARTIN: *(off)* Not another one!

ELISE: *(loud)* We are about to possess a home of our own. I mean a *real* home, what do you say to that?

MARTIN: *(off)* The others weren't real?

ELISE: *(loud)* They weren't *ours. (Quieter)* The husband owns title, don't ask me why. Hus-*bands.* When love goes wrong, we don't stoop to payoffs—I don't, anyway. Pride. *Tant pis pour moi.*

MARTIN: *(off)* I can't hear you.

(ELISE *flips through magazines, circling an item, dog-earing a page, etc.)*

ELISE: Aren't you sick of all this moving around? Wouldn't it be lovely to live somewhere spacious and light and permanent where I could get back to my poetry and you had your own room for . . . well, whatever. What are you up to out there, plotting the Revolution?

MARTIN: *(off)* Of course, what else?

ELISE: *(smiles)* You see, it's all to do with these new materials they developed for the war. Now they're looking like mad for peacetime markets, like house-building—only contractors won't use anything new until it's proven, and how can you prove it till you use it. And *that*, my dear, is where we come in . . .

MARTIN: *(reenters with milk bottle half full)* This is all I could find.

ELISE: Milk! What luck, my absolutely favorite meal. You can live for years on nothing else, did you know that?

MARTIN: It's warm.

ELISE: As nature intended. Did you ever hear of a refrigerated cow?

MARTIN: Is the icebox broken, too?

ELISE: No, angel, there is nothing wrong with the icebox.
    Or the fan, for that matter. It's the electric company, I
    don't know what is the matter with those people . . .

MARTIN: *(flipping wall switch)* The power's been discon-
    nected?

ELISE: It was that or the phone. And since nothing excit-
    ing ever entered my life through the icebox, I paid the
    phone bill.

MARTIN: Mom, what do you live on?

ELISE: *(snippy)* On the fact that I'm putting you through
    school and you'll have opportunities I never had. What
    a shame my Little Lord Fauntleroy missed the Depres-
    sion, or he wouldn't be so quick to judge his own flesh
    and blood . . .

MARTIN: Okay, take it easy, all I meant . . . never mind.

ELISE: What, angel? You're such a Moody Morris. I
    thought my little ambassador would come home glow-
    ing with triumph.

MARTIN: I guess I'm just tired. It's a long train ride down.
    Tell me your idea, I'll get the glasses for dinner.

(ELISE *watches his exit to kitchen. Something is up.*)

ELISE: I'm approaching all the manufacturers with a
    proposition: They contribute their most controversial
    products from which I'll offer to design and build The

Home of The Future. They get a free showcase, we get a free house, and free enterprise triumphs once again.

MARTIN: *(reenters, holding two mismatched glasses to the light to check for dirt)* What do we build this house on?

ELISE: On a piece of land, silly head, what else?

MARTIN: And where do we get this piece of land?

ELISE: In the fullness of time, all will be revealed: Sunday night.

MARTIN: What's the big deal about Sunday, just tell me.

ELISE: *(teasing)* Curiosity killed the cat.

MARTIN: Mom, it's just another pipe dream.

ELISE: *Pipe dream?* Where on earth do you pick up these curious expressions?

MARTIN: You know what it means.

ELISE: *Une rêve du pipe?* Is that, for instance, when you send your son to one of the best progressive schools in the east and he's failing nearly every subject at mid-year? *(Teasingly)* Plus caught drinking in the science lab? And taking the school jeep on a midnight joy ride over very dangerous logging trails which nearly got him expelled, not to mention killed—and I hope you know how much I'd save having you at a public school here in the city—but no, the mother pesters and pleads till the headmaster gives him one last chance, all because she

has this *pipe dream* he'll end up with an A-minus average, write a brilliant essay and be chosen as the school's
first exchange student ever . . . is that what you mean
by a pipe dream?

MARTIN: Why *did* you leave me up there? How come you
didn't just bring me home?

ELISE: I feel innuendo peeking through the window.
What are you trying to say, angel mine?

MARTIN: I'm not *trying* to say anything. I asked a question, you obviously don't want to answer, and that's the
end of that.

ELISE: *Mais quelle force! Quelle finalité. Je suis desolé.*
(Smiles) Did you understand?

MARTIN: Why should I?

ELISE: Darling, you're not off to Switzerland as a tourist,
you represent a school, an entire nation, you must be
fluent in the language.

MARTIN: That was French, Mom. The Swiss speak German.

ELISE: *(snaps)* Don't lecture me about the Swiss. I knew a
dwarf from Zurich once. He spoke French. To me, anyway.

MARTIN: Why do you say these stupid things when you
don't know what you're talking about . . . !

ELISE: *(grandly)* Switzerland is a mountainous country full of very clean people who stayed neuter in the war. They eat lots of chocolate and always know what time it is. If they want to speak German, that's their problem.

MARTIN: Neutral, Mom. They were *neutral* in the war.

ELISE: That's what I said.

MARTIN: You said neuter.

ELISE: A pedant, no less. (MARTIN *starts out)* Where do you think you're going?

MARTIN: I have to get ready.

ELISE: Darling, I only have you for one short week. Let's both try hard to make the most of our time together. Sit.

(MARTIN *obeys.* ELISE *joins him and mimes that his head is a box with a lid she can unlock and open. An old game.)*

Now then; Turn the key/Open the lid/Look where all the secrets are hid . . . !

MARTIN: *(brushing her hand aside)* Don't.

ELISE: Do you want me to say I'm sorry? Is that really necessary? You know I wanted to be at Parent's Day. Imagine how I felt missing my son's finest hour, but we were weeks behind on the autumn line and they asked us to volunteer for overtime—which does not mean *volunteer,* it means which of you is truly dedicated to Maison de Maurice Continental Fashions. If I'd taken time off . . . you know how hard I've worked all year for promotion . . .

MARTIN: Are we ever going to see Andrew?

ELISE: Ah. So *that's* what this is all about.

MARTIN: We've been back in the city for almost a year.

ELISE: Shouldn't you be getting ready for your friends?

MARTIN: You always do this.

ELISE: Do what?

MARTIN: I bring up his name and, bang, you change the subject.

ELISE: There's nothing to say. He's not interested in us, *finis.*

MARTIN: How do you know?

ELISE: After ten years out west we return to his city and nothing, not a peep . . . *(Stops herself)* No, I swore I would never do this. I will not poison the well. I'm sure he has his reasons.

MARTIN: Was he the one who left?

ELISE: There was a war . . .

MARTIN: I mean after.

ELISE: Oh, who left who, what difference could it possibly make now? People change. He went away, he came back . . . different.

MARTIN: Why? What was he like before the war?

ELISE: *(beat)* Before the war . . . was a whole other world. Into the sunset, red flags waving, artists and workers of the world united.

MARTIN: *(trying to get it straight)* And I was . . . *after* that?

ELISE: You were never not there, my angel, my blessing.

MARTIN: Mom, I'm serious. . . .

ELISE: Darling, I've had a long day. Tomorrow. We'll have a nice talk tomorrow, all right?

MARTIN: What if he did want to see us?

ELISE: What if the moon was green cheese. He could have seen you on his own at Parent's Day if it's me he's afraid of.

MARTIN: He didn't know you wouldn't be there.

ELISE: That's hardly the point . . . what do you mean "he didn't know."

MARTIN: How could he, we haven't been in touch.

ELISE: You said he *didn't* know . . .

MARTIN: I said . . .

ELISE: Martin, look at me, I heard you.

MARTIN: You heard wrong.

ELISE: *(agitated)* Have you been in touch with him, has he called you at school, was he at Parent's Day?

MARTIN: Of course not. How could you even think something like that?

ELISE: I'm sorry, darling. You'd have told me, wouldn't you.

MARTIN: Cross my heart and hope to die, okay?

ELISE: No secrets. Not between the two of us.

MARTIN: It's only 'cause you said we'd all be together when we got back east . . .

ELISE: Never . . .

MARTIN: You did, Mom, when we left New Mexico, that first night in the motel . . .

ELISE: I said no such thing.

(Tired of this, MARTIN goes off to wash. ELISE is puzzled by his behavior. As she explains herself, we can see an edginess in her manner. First, she glances around to make sure he is gone then, talking, she removes flask from her

handbag, pours a slug of bourbon into her milk, sips and replaces flask in bag.)

I may have touched on the possibility of an evening together—something along those lines. I don't consider it extravagant of me to assume, after ten years, he might be just the least bit curious about . . . us. *(Quieter)* Who'd have thought he'd still be so terrified of contact.

MARTIN: *(breezes in combing hair)* Can I use your toothbrush? I left mine at school.

ELISE: What a handsome young man. You'll break some poor woman's heart one day. Not that one . . . !

(MARTIN *has lifted the wrong glass of milk. Pause. He brings it to his nose and smells, then sets it down.)*

ELISE: It's been a funny old year, darling. You see, I finally understand something, and it hasn't been easy. No one is going to help us. *(Brighter)* But when you return from Europe, we'll have our very own home, that's a promise. And we'll burn electricity till the wires hum hallelujah!

MARTIN: Mom.

ELISE: *(distant)* I thought I could leave this damn city behind.

MARTIN: *Mom.*

ELISE: What is it, angel?

MARTIN: I think the house is a great idea.

ELISE: *(beams)* In that case, I'm sure *some* people in Switzerland speak German. Prosit! *(Raises glass)* Now then, a warm bath, then slide between the sheets with a nice, fat Russian novel while my little genius slips into the night, with his mysterious friends from school. Undo me.

(MARTIN *hesitates, then unfastens his mother's dress down the back.*)

ELISE: *(sings)*
 I dreamed I saw Joe Hill last night
 alive as you or me
 says I, But Joe, you're ten years dead

MARTIN: *(joins)*
 I never died, says he
 I never died, says he . . .

ELSEWHERE (ANDREW'S PLACE)

(ANDREW *appears in a pool of light, watching something as he speaks.*)

ANDREW: *(like control tower)* Zurich, Switzerland to Inbound ST-107, do you read me . . .

ELISE: *(to* MARTIN*)* Thank you, angel . . .

ANDREW: Zurich, Switzerland to ST-107, come in . . .

ELISE: *(hugging* MARTIN*)* It's so nice to have company!

(ELISE *exits. Alone at last,* MARTIN *breathes deeply, as if relieved of a great weight. His arms go out like an airplane and, as lights dim on* ELISE's *place, he begins to fly across the stage in a shaft of light.*)

MARTIN: *(in flight)* ST-107 to Zurich Control, ST-107 to Zurich Control . . .

ANDREW: You have clearance to land, Runway two is your active, exit Green-C, that's "C" for Charlie, do you read . . . ?

MARTIN: *(in flight)* Active runway is two, exit Green-C, over and out . . .

(Lights up on ANDREW's *place, where* MARTIN *sits on packing box,* ANDREW *issuing commands. The room is bare, boxes around, a place being moved into. Among things being unpacked are books, a high-quality telescope, antique-model square rigger sailing ship, several crystal decanters, things of taste and elegance.* ANDREW *is an imposing man, forceful, energetic, used to giving orders and being listened to, but also capable of puzzling sudden delicacy of expression and manner, an almost pedantic fussiness.)*

ANDREW: Good, now what?

MARTIN: Left flap down, right rudder . . .

ANDREW: No, no, no, you approach Zurich from the *south* flying *west,* bank to the left . . .

MARTIN: Sorry, Dad, west, *west*—left flap *up*, left rudder, *right* flap down . . .

PENNY: *(breezes in)* Hey, poops, can I borrow your shaving brush . . . *(sees* MARTIN) Woops, sorry . . .

(PENNY *is in a bathrobe, pinning her hair up behind. She is in her early twenties.)*

ANDREW: Ah . . . Martin, this is Penny, my . . . friend. Penny, Martin.

PENNY: I didn't hear the door.

MARTIN: How do you do.

PENNY: Fine, thanks. What's up?

ANDREW: We're landing in Zurich.

PENNY: Should I fasten my seat belt? *(Starts out, stops)* Oh, is that okay, shaving brush?

ANDREW: Don't bang the water out, you loosen the hairs. Shake it dry. Shake it dry. *(Illustrates)*

PENNY: *(imitates, teasing)* Shake it dry.

(PENNY *exits, wiggling her bottom playfully . . .)*

Shake-it-dry, shake-it-dry . . .

(MARTIN *watches her exit with interest.* ANDREW *notes this and acts.)*

ANDREW: Deet-deet-deet, red light, emergency . . .

MARTIN: *(taken by surprise)* You said a routine landing . . .

ANDREW: You've gone red in the air, what do you do—full
throttle, get away from the ground as fast as you can,
and why is that?

MARTIN: I forgot . . .

ANDREW: 'Cause we're soft and . . .

BOTH: . . . the ground is hard, it's no contest!

ANDREW: Okay, I threw you a little zinger there. You did
well. Naaah, you did just great. Keep it up and we might
get you into a real machine this summer . . .

MARTIN: A DC-7?

ANDREW: Whoa! That's a big bird you're talking about.
Doubt I could fly one of those myself.

MARTIN: Why not, you're a pilot.

ANDREW: *(amused)* I'm a photographer, kiddo. I happen
to be shooting a spread for the airline, bummed a few
free lessons for the hell of it.

MARTIN: You're going to solo round the world, that's what
you said.

ANDREW: I said *maybe,* and till maybe happens, what do we call it?

MARTIN: A pipe dream.

ANDREW: There you go, now back to work . . .

MARTIN: But say we're flying to, I don't know, Switzerland or something, and there's an emergency, the pilot has a heart attack, you could take over and land, right?

ANDREW: There's a co-pilot.

MARTIN: He's epileptic.

ANDREW: I'd change airline. How 'bout less with the mouth and more with the hands.

(Both return to unpacking boxes.)

MARTIN: Great place. Kind of big for one person.

ANDREW: *(beat)* You don't mind that Penny joined us?

MARTIN: Why should I mind?

ANDREW: I'm glad you could make it over. Thought you'd have other plans, first night home from school.

MARTIN: Mom works late. It's a real hard job, lot of overtime.

ANDREW: She doesn't mind your dropping by?

MARTIN: I told you at Parent's Day, she's glad we're seeing each other. She appreciated your coming up to school when she's so busy. She wants us to spend time.

ANDREW: Sounds like she's changed.

MARTIN: She's pretty great. Talks about you all the time.

ANDREW: *(abruptly)* Open that box, I'll get us a Moxie, celebrate our first evening together, what do you say? *(Indicating box)* You'll find something inside—it's right on top. Had it framed.

MARTIN: *(holds up framed photo)* The cowboy? What for? Hey, this is *you!*

ANDREW: Lazy-Y Ranch.

MARTIN: You were a cowboy?

ANDREW: Well, I had a hat on my head and a horse under my butt, I guess so. And a fruit picker, sign painter, even deputy sheriff up in Idaho, you name it.

MARTIN: Mom never said.

ANDREW: Listen, kiddo. I quit school. I quit 'cause nothing made sense, what I saw going on around me—newspapers screaming prosperity, growth, record employment, while my dad and damn near everyone we knew could barely put meat on the table once a week, and still they believed the headlines. So, one day, bang, out the door, age fifteen, rode the rails west to see for myself, and you know what? After five years of knocking around, I knew the truth. The papers were lying. That's right. This country was a total Goddamn disaster. And they kept right on lying all the way to '29, when things got so bad they just couldn't anymore. You hold onto that *(the photo)* and remember—don't believe what they tell you. Go out and see for yourself. You know why I'm saying this?

MARTIN: Aren't we just talking?

ANDREW: I never "just talk." Think about it. I was in school; you're in school. I headed west; you're heading to Europe. Well?

MARTIN: *(puzzled)* Going away, is that what you mean?

ANDREW: I mean what's true and what's not true. I mean that essay of yours, the one you read at school.

MARTIN: The Cold War? What about it?

ANDREW: That's what I'd like to know. What about it?

MARTIN: *(still puzzled)* It won the contest. *(Brighter)* They're gonna publish it in *Roots and Branches,* that's the yearbook. I can save you a copy.

(MARTIN *is trying to slip out of this, lifting box to carry elsewhere.)*

ANDREW: Look at me, Marty. Tell me how it went.

MARTIN: I didn't memorize it, Dad. "The Cold War is both a war and not a war," something like that . . .

ANDREW: Keep going.

MARTIN: You heard it at Parent's Day.

ANDREW: Refresh my memory.

MARTIN: "It is two great powers, Russia and America, pitting their citizens against each other with propaganda, lies and silence . . ."

ANDREW: To me, Marty, to *me*.

MARTIN: *(braving it)* "But perhaps we have more in common than we know. Take our very initials, U.S. and U.S.S.R., both begin with *us*, and does this not suggest a greater unity . . ."

ANDREW: Good, you're blushing . . .

MARTIN: I am not.

ANDREW: It's bullshit, and you know it. You're just parroting back what you know they want to hear up at that circus of a school, "International Brotherhood of Man" . . . Christ alive . . .

MARTIN: Take it easy, that's just the motto . . .

ANDREW: It's a wet dream for radical has-beens. They hire a staff of academic rejects from around the world—at half price—and call it a *Global Environment.* How could she get suckered in, after everything we fought for back then.

MARTIN: Look, if you don't like the place, why don't you call Mom and we'll all get together and talk it over.

ANDREW: *(beat)* Knowledge is everything, Marty. Everything. I don't want to see you open your mouth ever again to please another man. You say only what you truly believe, or you shut up.

MARTIN: Dad, what if . . . say I hadn't written that essay.

ANDREW: Did you?

MARTIN: Sort of. Not really. I cribbed it from this U.N. journal in the school library. I didn't mean for it to get all out of hand like this. *(Beat)* Dad?

ANDREW: All right. Put it out of your head. I don't think you're that kind of kid. Are you?

MARTIN: I thought they'd catch me. I thought I'd be sent home. Someone has to be with her.

ANDREW: Who? Wait a minute. You tried to get yourself booted on her account?

MARTIN: *(agitated)* She pretends everything's okay, but I know she doesn't mean it, not this time, or maybe it's just different now 'cause it was always, before, when we moved someplace she'd make it a big adventure and it was all going to be fine, but nothing's working out the way she planned and I don't know how to make it better—she doesn't eat right, she gives her money away,

she forgets to pay her bills and now I'll be gone all
year . . .

ANDREW: Stop right there. That woman is tough as old
leather, and always has been. She doesn't want help.
People have tried, believe me. You carry your own load,
Martin. She'll be fine. Do you understand me?

MARTIN: Yes, sir.

ANDREW: Now let's have that Moxie.

PENNY: *(reenters, still in robe)* Okay, last time, I promise.
Toothbrush?

ANDREW: Sorry, kitten, you're out of luck.

MARTIN: I have one. *(Takes it out)* Look, still sealed.

PENNY: You always carry that around, talk about ready for
anything. I shouldn't, but since he won't let me keep
one here . . .

ANDREW: Hey, mischief . . . !

MARTIN: Take it, I'll buy a whole new one tomorrow. The
city's full of toothbrushes, I checked.

PENNY: You checked? Listen to the comedian.

MARTIN: It's extra–stiff bristle, is that okay?

PENNY: I wouldn't have it any other way.

ANDREW: Let's hop into something decent, dinner's on the way.

PENNY: Tell ya what, just for being such a sugar-pie, I'm going to get you a little something of my own for Europe and give it to you at the party Sunday . . .

MARTIN: Party, what party?

ANDREW: Penny, some clothes . . .

PENNY: You haven't told . . . woops.

ANDREW: *(to* MARTIN, *off-hand)* Just a little wing-ding to show off the new campsite here, maybe stir up a little wind about this new photo magazine I'm thinking of starting . . .

PENNY: Sure, poops, on Father's Day?!

ANDREW: Wasn't the invitation supposed to come *after* dinner?

PENNY: *That's* the part I forgot.

ANDREW: Miss Nervous here. *(To* MARTIN) If you can make it. Pretty lively crowd shaping up. I know it's your last night in town. I don't want to cause any trouble at the other end.

MARTIN: Sunday?

PENNY: Seven o'clock on . . .

MARTIN: I'll have to let you know.

ANDREW: Either way, no big deal. Sort of last minute thing . . . *(doorbell)* There's the Chinaman, rustle up some dishes, that box . . . *(exits)*

(MARTIN, *left alone with* PENNY, *busies himself with a box.)*

PENNY: You're a real sweetheart helping with the move, it means a lot to Andrew. *(Lifts a thick book)* Chinese dictionary. Typical, the old slyboots—one minute he's Mister-Regular-Guy, next thing he's jabbering away with a waiter in Chinese. "Oh, you know, I picked it up here and there." Are you like that, know tons of stuff and never let on? Like with this party—and don't let him fool you, the whole thing's for you, he's been acting like a ten–year–old ever since you got in touch. Hey, I have a terrific idea, let's make this a conversation.

MARTIN: Are you in love with my father?

PENNY: Oh, small talk, my favorite kind. You're a very intense young man. Nice, but intense. Andrew and I are having a very fun time together, yes.

MARTIN: That's not what I asked.

PENNY: And this isn't exactly the conversation I imagined having with my boyfriend's son.

MARTIN: Boy? He's old enough to be your father.

PENNY: Are we getting along or not?

MARTIN: Are we supposed to?

PENNY: Have it your way . . . *(moves to go)*

MARTIN: Do you love him?

PENNY: That's none of your business. *(Gentler)* He keeps it simple, and simple is what I happen to want right now —clean, wholesome fun, and no strings. Like the animals I work with—grrr-grrr, slither-slither, sniff-sniff, "Hello, beastie, I like you, let's play."

MARTIN: *(laughs)* You're nuts.

PENNY: You got a great smile, kid. You ought to use it more.

MARTIN: I'm not a kid.

PENNY: You know what I think? There's two kinds of Martin, they change by the hour, one of them's sweet, the other one's sour.

MARTIN: There's more than two of me. A lot more.

PENNY: Ooooow, mystery, chills-up-my-spine!

ANDREW: *(reenters with Chinese food)* Hey, chop-chop, a little movement in the clothing department.

PENNY: Now there's the big problem, sugar, nothing to wear.

ANDREW: Cut the games, Penny, not tonight.

PENNY: It's the god's honest truth, we've been cleaning the hippo compound, and when I went to shower the locker was jammed shut, and you wanted me here early to help with the move, so I had no time to go home and change . . .

ANDREW: All right, check the closet, take something of mine.

PENNY: See what I mean, if I just kept a few things here . . .

ANDREW: End of story . . .

PENNY: I'm not being devious, honeybun. No anchors are being dropped in your harbor.

ANDREW: Penelope . . .

PENNY: *Penny.* I hate that name.

ANDREW: *Clothes.*

PENNY: *(to* MARTIN*)* He's so cute when he's angry. *(Exits)*

ANDREW: *(beat)* Loves to stir it up, that one. Every angle.

MARTIN: Are you going to marry her?

ANDREW: Penny? Marry her? *(Chuckles)* Damn interesting gal, though. Saving up for field work in Africa, Thompson's gazelle, migration, some such. Self-taught . . . why?

MARTIN: *(suddenly)* I've made up my mind, Dad. I'm coming to the party.

ANDREW: *(caught off-guard, delighted)* Yeah? You sure, now? Aw, Marty, that's dandy, that's just . . . hey, I'm tickled pink—this calls for a drink. Damn it, the Moxie, went clean out of my head. *(Exits)*

MARTIN: *(calls)* Can I bring someone?

ANDREW: *(off)* It's your bash, kiddo. Yours and mine. School buddy? Girlfriend? *(Reenters)* Hey, you got yourself a little steady up there . . . what's her name?

ELSEWHERE (ELISE'S PLACE)

(Enter ELISE, *dancing a sensuous, dramatic tango to music from next door. She wears a high-fashion gown, circa mid-1950s.)*

MARTIN: I think you'll like her.

ANDREW: If she's your friend, she's mine.

ELISE: *(to someone offstage)* Dance, my dear, is ninety percent style, and style is ninety percent confidence. Just think: Tallulah!

MARTIN: What are you going to do with all this room, Dad?

ANDREW: Fill it full of whatever the hell I want. *(Enter* PENNY *in outsize clothes of* ANDREW's) And here she is, let's dust off some dishes and tie on the feed bag . . .

(As lights fade on ANDREW*'s place,* EMMA *enters to* ELISE, *dancing an awkward tango and wearing a pink gown that looks ludicrous on her petite, rotund body.)*

ELISE: *(encouraging* EMMA*'s efforts)* Perfect, my dear, you'll be an absolute sensation tonight . . .

EMMA: I feel like a strawberry cupcake in a straitjacket, it's no use, Elise, I can't dance, I can't breathe, and my tush looks three sizes too big in this ridiculous contraption.

ELISE: Nonsense, you have a perfectly lovely Boticelli figure.

EMMA: Just my luck to be born four centuries late.

ELISE: A century early, like me, but until our time, we'll carry the flame by living as unspeakably as two men.

EMMA: *(giggles)* You're *terrible.*

ELISE: . . . And don't you love it.

(Enter LEW *from the kitchen, holding a bottle of bourbon, half gone. He is a powerful, gentle man in his mid-twenties.)*

LEW: Glasses?

ELISE: Try the sink. (LEW *exits)* What's his name again?

EMMA: Lewis something, I think he said.

ELISE: Tsk, tsk, tsk, you naughty person. *(Music has stopped) (calling towards wall) Once More, Prudencia, Por Favor. (To* EMMA*)* She gets her records from South America, how I love that Latin yearning . . . *(vamping in the silence)*

EMMA: Are we really going out in these? What if someone recognizes the style?

ELISE: They'll have a sneak preview of the Maison de Maurice autumn formals.

EMMA: But if you're caught! It seems so reckless after how hard you've worked for promotion.

ELISE: They'll be back in the showroom long before they're missed, now stop worrying my darling Conscience, this is our night of the week, and damn the rules. *(Music has begun again)* Now there's a woman who understands! *(Calls) Grazia, Signora,* or whatever it is in South American—this time you lead.

*(*ELISE *sweeps* EMMA *up in a dance,* EMMA *blushing.* MARTIN *enters and watches for a moment.)*

EMMA: Nooo . . . *(giggling)*

MARTIN: Hi, everyone, lady's night out. Where'd you get those?

ELISE: *(dances over)* Hello there, mysterious stranger, don't I know you from somewhere . . . ?

MARTIN: *(gently changing the game) Hi, Emma.*

(EMMA, *who has been adjusting the back of her gown, spins around startled.*)

EMMA: My God! *(recovering)* I'm sorry.

MARTIN: Did I say something?

EMMA: Your voice, it's exactly like . . . It's gotten so husky since mid-year . . .

MARTIN: Who is it like?

ELISE: *(cutting in)* Join us, angel. Tell Emma she's thin in German.

EMMA: Isn't it exciting, a whole year in Switzerland! All that culture—and snow!

ELISE: And what has the mystery man been up to?

MARTIN: Nothing.

ELISE: Now doesn't that conjure a vivid picture, yes, I see it all . . .

MARTIN: I have to change. By the way, Mom, you know on Sunday.

ELISE: *(quick)* What about Sunday?

MARTIN: Nothing, I was just wondering—have you made any actual plan-plans?

ELISE: Every minute of the evening is accounted for, why?

MARTIN: Nothing. *(Starts off)*

ELISE: "Nothing." Must be the new word of the fifties. And while we're at it, kindly remove your dirty laundry from the floor in there. I am not here to peel grapes for the Sultan of Bumbum.

(LEW *has entered and stands in doorway.)*

LEW: Don't let me interrupt . . .

ELISE: Say hello to Lewis, he's a friend of Emma's.

EMMA: *(absurdly)* Lew is from Witchita . . . didn't you say?

LEW: Yes, ma'm. Sunshine State of Kansas.

MARTIN: *(shakes hands with* LEW) Hi. See ya. *(Exits)*

LEW: Thing is, your fridge seems kind of warm, you keep the ice anywhere special?

ELISE: The day is far too hot for ice, Lew. Just pour and carry. (LEW *exits)* Does Martin really sound that much like . . .

EMMA: I'm sorry, I couldn't help myself. The way he said "Hi, Emma" . . .

ELISE: He's certainly developing Andrew's manner. Imperious, full of disapproving looks. He blames me that his father hasn't been in touch, but what more can I do, I told him we were coming east . . .

EMMA: You spoke to Andrew?

ELISE: Post card, hello-goodbye. Emma, I need a favor, a very big one.

EMMA: How big is very?

ELISE: I bought some land. An entire acre.

EMMA: When? Where?

ELISE: Upstate, by a river somewhere.

EMMA: You haven't seen it?

ELISE: An inside deal, there wasn't time. I need a mortgage by the weekend, or the whole thing goes on public auction.

EMMA: How much?

ELISE: It won't be touched. Straight into my savings account, and when the upstate bank sees my collateral, I get the mortgage, and you get back every penny.

EMMA: You know I can't refuse you anything. So please don't ask unless you're sure you know what you're doing.

ELISE: Would you think me crazy if I told you that for the first time in years I feel *lucky.* Look how well Martin is doing—I'm reestablished in the city—I even started a new poem. And guess what? I didn't get the promotion.

EMMA: How can that be, they promised!

ELISE: Office intrigue, tushes unkissed. And not a word to Martin—nothing darkens this week of ours.

EMMA: All that overtime, the weekends, aren't you crushed?

ELISE: Not a bit, that's the whole point. I know what I really want now, and the rest is just weather, a few clouds, a light sprinkle, who cares. I've had my revenge, we're wearing it.

EMMA: Bring it to the union. File a complaint . . .

ELISE: . . . Sunday night I'm taking Martin to dinner, then "My Fair Lady"—yes, a special show for the union, I got front row center . . . balcony . . . and afterwards, by taxi to the Hawaiian Room where I've ordered champagne waiting, and as we raise our glasses to toast, I shall hand Martin the deed to an entire acre of land by a river in both our names—oh, Emma, I can't wait to see his face!

EMMA: You are crazy. Or the most resilient woman on earth.

ELISE: "Over a sea of endless sorrow/On we sail with reckless joy." That's the start of my new poem.

EMMA: The answer is yes—of course. If I have it. And it's what you really want.

ELISE: *(sweeps* EMMA *into an impulsive dance of joy)* Darling Emma, sweet-wonderful-Emma, how did I manage for ten years away from you?

EMMA: Stop! Elise! No, I can't!

LEW: *(enters, two glasses in hand)* Rumba-dumba, lead me to the party.

EMMA: Lew! Oh, God, I forgot, you're here.

LEW: Two things; A: I like what I see and B, you might have yourself an electric problem in the kitchen—flashlight and a screwdriver, I'll have a looksee.

ELISE: The condition is temporary and minor, thanks all the same.

LEW: *(extends glasses)* Down the hatch.

EMMA: That's enough for ten people, Lew. We haven't even eaten yet.

(LEW *gulps down most of one glassful and reextends glass to* EMMA.)

LEW: Try that.

ELISE: Who said chivalry was dead. *(Takes other glass)*

LEW: This Greenwich Village is quite a proposition. How's about that place on the corner with the black toilet in the window. Kinda off-beat touch for a restaurant.

ELISE: Lew, may I ask you a direct question?

LEW: It's a free country.

ELISE: Who on earth *are* you, and why did you follow Emma here?

LEW: That's pretty direct.

EMMA: I don't normally attach myself to strange men in the street.

LEW: Am I that strange?

ELISE: To be found drifting in our bohemian latitudes, a little, yes. You strike me as a man with a more regular sort of wife—life, I mean, *life*.

LEW: If I'm a third wheel here, just say the word and I'll roll on down the road.

EMMA: Were you part of the demonstration or not?

LEW: I was following my nose, sight-seeing is all. Heard women yelling out the windows, I look up and see bars, hell, couldn't believe it. Where I come from you don't put a woman's prison smack dab in the middle of town. Then I see Emma and them down below with banners

—I figure in the way of local color it's got the Circle Line beat all to hell.

ELISE: *(amused)* We seem to have a slight misunderstanding.

LEW: No, ma'm, I understand when it feels real nice talking with someone.

EMMA: Lew was a frogman . . . isn't that what you said?

LEW: *(shows tattoo on arm)* Korea.

ELISE: And how many tadpoles did you leave behind, Lew?

LEW: Beg pardon? Oh, I get it. *(Smiles)* Like if I had some kids out of wedlock. Pretty sneaky how you put that, sneaks up on you.

ELISE: Haven't you a glass?

LEW: In there? *(Points to kitchen)* Refill anyone?

ELISE: Oh, bend my arm. *(Extends her glass grandly)*

EMMA: I'm fine, thank you.

LEW: If you don't mind my saying so, you're a helluva lot better than fine, Emma. *(Exits to kitchen)*

EMMA: *(blushing at ELISE's amusement)* Oh, God, how could I bring him here, what was I thinking?

ELISE: He's sweet, he's good looking and he likes you. Perhaps my luck is rubbing off on a friend.

EMMA: No, no, it's too bizarre, what could he possibly want with a woman like me?

ELISE: Three guesses.

EMMA: Stop. Men never walk up to me like that—with a big smile, unless . . . *(realizes)* Oh my God, oh no . . . !

ELISE: What?

EMMA: That's exactly how they penetrate, find a demonstration . . .

ELISE: What on earth are you talking about?

EMMA: The F.B.I.

ELISE: *Emma!*

EMMA: Sure, sure, you think it all ended with Senator McCarthy, but you're wrong. Cedric's been getting mysterious phone calls upstairs. They listen and hang up. He's sure they're watching our building, and everyone knows I take his mail when he travels . . .

ELISE: . . . And they all know he was in our commune twenty years ago, oh yes, Cedric among the rustic revolutionaries, poison ivy from head to foot, *Das Kapital* in hand, sowing corn for the masses. Popping corn. I assure you, the F.B.I. did not tremble at our labors.

EMMA: It's been so long since I was with a man—*that* way.

ELISE: Like riding a bicycle. Once you mount, the rest comes rushing back.

EMMA: You're *terrible.*

MARTIN: *(enters)* Anyone for the bathroom? I'm going to take a shower.

ELISE: Darling, guess what, due to a sudden change of plan, your mother is free as a bird tonight . . .

EMMA: You can't leave me alone with that man!

ELISE: Shush.

MARTIN: Sorry, Mom, tonight I'm booked.

ELISE: The mystery friends from school, no doubt.

MARTIN: *(beat)* Would you like to meet them?

ELISE: Me? You're asking your mother along to share your secret life?

MARTIN: There's a party Sunday.

ELISE: Sunday?

MARTIN: They planned this whole going-to-Europe thing for me. It was supposed to be a surprise.

ELISE: I'm sorry, dear, Sunday is out of the question.

MARTIN: Come on, Mom, it'll be great, they said I could bring someone. You always talk about meeting my friends, well, now's your chance.

ELISE: Martin, there will be no discussion about this. We made a date, it's final.

MARTIN: How about if we just dropped in for a little while.

ELISE: I said no. If it's that important, tell them to have it in the afternoon.

MARTIN: How can they just change everything at the last minute?

ELISE: Oh, *they* can't but *I* can.

EMMA: Excuse me, I'll just help Lew in the kitchen . . . *(she doesn't move)*

MARTIN: The party's for me, Mom. You're not going to let me go to my own party?

ELISE: Honestly, you are the limit. You come breezing in and expect me to rearrange my life at your every whim.

MARTIN: No, Mom, if I said I was going to Parent's Day, I'd go.

ELISE: That was unworthy of you.

EMMA: Please excuse me . . . *(she stays put)*

MARTIN: Forget it, all right, let's just forget the whole thing . . . *(starts out)*

ELISE: You turn around and march yourself right back in here, young man . . .

MARTIN: It's my party, and I'm going, with or without you.

ELISE: You do demand your pound of flesh.

MARTIN: *(relenting)* All I meant . . . they never got a chance to meet you at school. You were busy, I understand, but you're free Sunday night, and I'd just be really proud if I could introduce you.

ELISE: *(beat)* Mister Tongue of Velvet. But afterwards, I demand a private hour alone with his majesty.

MARTIN: You'll get all dressed up, okay? Like you do sometimes?

ELISE: I shall not disappoint.

LEW: *(enters with empty bottle)* We got us a dead soldier here. I'll spring for a live one if you like.

EMMA: We've had more than enough, Lew.

MARTIN: Sorry I yelled. And thanks. Have a good old time . . . everyone. *(Moves to go)*

LEW: *(to* MARTIN*)* I see you're looking at the critter.

MARTIN: The what?

LEW: *(exposing tattoo)* Bet you never seen one of these jobbies before.

MARTIN: A tattoo? I have, actually.

LEW: Not like this. See, the upper half's a man.

MARTIN: So it is.

LEW: How 'bout below the waist? I got me a watch right here says you can't guess what it is.

MARTIN: A frog.

LEW: *(beat)* I'll be darned. Smart hombre.

MARTIN: The web feet sort of give it away.

LEW: *(removing watch)* Whole outfit got 'em. Inchon Harbor, little Chinee fellow, two different color eyes. *(Holds out his watch)* There ya go.

ELISE: Lew, that's hardly appropriate.

LEW: A bet's a bet. Won it in a poker game to start with, easy come, easy go.

EMMA: *(agitated)* Lew, would you please put that back on and stop behaving this way.

MARTIN: Should I stick around, Mom?

ELISE: Take your shower.

(MARTIN *exits. Pause.*)

LEW: He's your son? I thought it was more one of those brother-sister type things, you hardly look old enough . . .

ELISE: Lewis, are you in some kind of trouble?

LEW: *(awkward)* I'll just pop on downstairs for another bottle. You might want to give the electrical folks a call, I think you've been shut off. *(Beat)* I didn't realize there was families involved here. *(Exits)*

EMMA: This is not a stable man. Now what do we do, he knows where you live.

ELISE: He won't be back.

EMMA: How do you know?

ELISE: He left his wife recently. Or vice versa. I've made an informal study of men in his condition.

EMMA: So much for *my* luck. Shall we eat? I'm famished.

ELISE: Emma, I love you dearly. We'll always be together, won't we—eat, dance, grow old together, two leftover lefties in tennis shoes and sweat socks . . .

EMMA: I think I'll wear a cape—a black one!

ELISE: Yes, and we'll carry umbrellas, and if anyone is rude to us, we'll whack them on the ankles . . .

MARTIN: *(off) Last call for the bathroom* . . .

ELISE: I want the money. I'm asking you for it here and now. He'll see that I can carry through. That his strength comes from me.

(EMMA *removes a checkbook from her handbag, signs and tears out a check, then holds open the ledger page for* ELISE.)

EMMA: That's my balance. Make it out for whatever you need.

ELISE: What do you really think, Emma?

EMMA: I think you have an extraordinary heart. I think you love better than you know.

ELISE: Dear Emma. Be close to me always . . . always.

(LEW *stands in the doorway, sheepish. Both see him at the same time.)*

LEW: I feel like a damn heel, slinking off like that. May I come in for a minute?

ELISE: I think Lew has something to tell us.

EMMA: Stop doing this, first you're inside, then you're outside, then you're back inside . . .

LEW: I know, I know . . .

EMMA: Stay put, just stay in one place until we're used to it . . . *(gulps down drink)*

LEW: My fault, I didn't mean to upset you . . . *(advances into room)* Fact is, I don't know what the hell I'm doing any more. See, it looks a little like I might be leaving my wife. (ELISE *and* EMMA *exchange a look)* Came here for the expo, but that closed a few days back and I'm still here, floating around. We been gearing up to start on our own, me and my partner back home, Luigi, which happens to be Lew in Eye-talian. My card. (LEW *passes his business card to* EMMA, *who reads it out loud)*

EMMA: "How can you lose when you use Two Lews . . ."

LEW: The slogan's more my idea. Needed something catchy.

ELISE: *(takes card and reads out)* "Contracting, renovation, modernizing, no job too big." *(Beat)* You're a builder, Lew?

LEW: That's the plan. Bank's in. Made a ton of contacts at the Housing Show. Everyone seems to think we'll do real good. Only problem is, my heart's just not in it, which how can you tell people when they're rooting for you all the way . . .

ELISE: *(passes her drink to* LEW) Go on, Lewis, the natives are friendly.

LEW: *(beat)* I been sleeping out in Central Park. Kind of an impulse–type thing. But I tell you, I haven't felt so damn happy since Korea. Like I was thinking, here I am, lying on my back in the middle of this great city on what's gotta be the most valuable piece of real estate going, but no one builds there. It's free for everyone to enjoy. Now doesn't that say something about people at their best. *(Shy)* I say that kinda stuff back home and they look at me like I got a lump on my head the size of a grapefruit. Anyhow, that's my story. *(Drains glass)* Thanks for hearing me out. *(Moves to leave)*

ELISE: Lew, I think it's remarkable that you should happen along tonight. Please, allow us to buy you dinner, and ask you questions, and grow wise.

EMMA: Elise . . . !

ELISE: The house.

EMMA: My goodness, yes. What luck!

ELISE: When it rains, it pours.

ELSEWHERE (CENTRAL PARK)

(Enter PENNY in soiled zoo coveralls, looking for someone whom she spots in the distance.)

PENNY: *(calls)* Martin!

LEW: I hope you don't think this is all some kind of fancy line I'm handing you. I see how it must look, what I'm up to . . .

ELISE: *(applying make-up)* We're big girls, Lew. Eyes open wide . . . et cetera.

PENNY: *(calls, waving)* Yoo-hoo, over here!

LEW: I can't believe my luck running into the two of you.

ELISE: Yes, things seem to be looking up all around. *(Calls) Don't be too late, Darling!*

PENNY: *(calls)* Over the footbridge!

ELISE: *(grandly, from doorway) Avanti!*

(ELISE, EMMA and LEW exit and lights go down on ELISE's place as MARTIN enters to PENNY in Central Park, with a shopping bag.)

MARTIN: I got lost after the Sheep Meadow, sorry.

PENNY: They owe me a long lunch. You like my spot?

MARTIN: It's like being in the country.

PENNY: I sleep out here sometimes. The park's full of people at night. You can hear 'em in the bushes.

MARTIN: *(removes food from bag)* Cheese and bread, is that okay?

PENNY: It was sweet of you to suggest this. After the other night, I wasn't sure where we stood.

MARTIN: I didn't expect someone so young. And pretty.

PENNY: If that's a compliment, I accept. *(She watches as* MARTIN *removes wine and a blanket.)* Wine! Aren't we French! But red? I believe for picnics in the park with your father's girlfriend, the wine of choice is white.

MARTIN: *(puzzled)* There's no such thing.

PENNY: I'm joshing. I see we have the serious Martin today.

MARTIN: *(takes wine)* I'll open it.

PENNY: You want to know a secret? Andrew has every single letter you ever wrote to him, all the way back to baby scrawl when he was overseas.

MARTIN: He told you that?

PENNY: I snooped. How else do you learn about Andrew? In the night table. I spend the night sometimes. Does that shock you?

MARTIN: I figured it went beyond Chinese food.

PENNY: Touché.

MARTIN: How come you're telling me this?

PENNY: An olive branch. You offer bread and wine, I offer a peek behind the Throne of Glory.

(Pause. MARTIN *notices* PENNY *watching him.)*

MARTIN: What are you looking at?

PENNY: *(beat)* You know—sometimes at the zoo, and no one's figured out why—this very peculiar thing happens. Bang, out of nowhere, the animals go berserk—bellow, screech, rattle the cages, throw themselves at each other. And then, just as suddenly, they go absolutely quiet. You can almost hear their hearts beating. It's as if they'd been in the grip of some wild, overwhelming passion, and now they're embarrassed by their own feelings. *(Beat)* People are animals. *(Beat)* Do you know what I'm saying?

MARTIN: *(looks away)* Wine?

PENNY: So what's this all about?

MARTIN: All what?

PENNY: Some people just can't fake it with each other. It's cards on the table, or nothing.

MARTIN: It's about the party. I have a problem.

PENNY: That's better. See how easy it is?

MARTIN: I'm bringing someone.

PENNY: And . . . ?

MARTIN: And . . . see, at school there's a lot of kids from the city. Which means stories get back sometimes, you know, like about our parents and everything. And that's real bad news, 'cause it's supposed to be you keep your home life kind of quiet.

PENNY: How come?

MARTIN: Oh, the old story, all of us sent away from home, sort of let's-not-talk-about-why.

PENNY: Ah, *that* old story.

MARTIN: Please don't take this the wrong way . . .

PENNY: I'm listening.

MARTIN: See, if word got back that my father dated real young girls . . . they can really make your life hell with gossip like that.

PENNY: You mean stop dating Andrew because it embarrasses you?

MARTIN: Don't be silly. It's just my date . . . she's from school, really nice girl, but she's got a big mouth and if she saw you with Andrew . . .

PENNY: What are you getting at?

MARTIN: Like if you couldn't make it Sunday night? There's a flu bug going around.

PENNY: *(laughs)* This is the first time I've ever been hustled by an adolescent.

MARTIN: It's no joke, Penny. One kid had a nervous breakdown when it got back his mom was a hooker . . .

PENNY: I know my overalls stink, but I can still smell bullshit when a truckload of it falls on my head. The answer is no, N-O . . .

ELSEWHERE (ELISE'S PLACE)

(ELISE *bustles on in a morning rush, coffee mug, cigarette, hairbrush, calling towards bathroom.*)

ELISE: Martin, hurry up in there. What are you doing, plotting the Revolution?

MARTIN: *(to* PENNY, *urgently)* Just this once, it's the only favor I'll ever ask.

PENNY: I don't know what your game is, but count me out. You should study your father, Martin. God knows he has his faults, but he always plays straight . . . *(starts off)*

ELISE: Martin!

MARTIN: *(to* PENNY*)* Don't tell him we met . . . Penny!

(PENNY *is gone.* MARTIN *circles to* ELISE*'s place and enters.*)

ELISE: Martin . . . there you are, God, what a dawdler, I'm centuries late for work . . .

MARTIN: On Sunday?

ELISE: Fashion waits for no man—keep an eye on the coffee pot—*(holds out mug)* here, take this, and do me up in back, will you?

MARTIN: Mom, we have to talk . . .

ELISE: *(bustling around)* After work, meet me here at five and we'll grab a quick bite before the party, make it five-thirty. . . . *(Exits)*

MARTIN: There is no party. It's been called off.

ELISE: *(beat, off)* I'm sure I heard that wrong.

MARTIN: I made it all up. There is no party.

ELISE: *(reenters, furious)* Martin, you can't do this to me, I cancelled all our plans, I gave away tickets to a Broadway show.

MARTIN: I've been seeing Andrew.

ELISE: *(pause)* Oh. *(Pause)* Since when?

MARTIN: Parent's Day.

ELISE: Of course. He's the one you wanted to be with tonight.

MARTIN: I'll be with you.

ELISE: Isn't it Father's Day?

MARTIN: Yes, Mom, we both know what day it is. You think I didn't know why you were making such a big deal about tonight . . .

ELISE: That was unworthy of you.

ELISE: It's been a funny old year, darling. You see, I finally understand something, and it hasn't been easy. No one is going to help us. (*brighter*) But when you return from Europe, we'll have our very own home, that's a promise. And we'll burn electricity till the wires hum hallelujah!

(At left, Kate Nelligan as Elise; Christopher Collet as Martin)
Photo Credit: Susan Cook

ELISE: Dance, my dear, is ninety percent style, and style is ninety percent confidence. Just think: Tallulah!

(At left, Alice Playten as Emma; center, Kate Nelligan as Elise; at right, Christopher Collet as Martin)
Photo Credit: Susan Cook

ANDREW: Listen, kiddo, I had a thought. How'd you like a little company on the trip over?

MARTIN: You mean Europe?

ANDREW: Leave early, take a few weeks, Burma, Chinese border, show you some of the old army haunts, maybe shoot a travel piece coffee table stuff, then drop you off in Switzerland.

MARTIN: Just you and me?

ANDREW: Spend some time. Catch up.

MARTIN: Mom's never been abroad.

ANDREW: Us, Marty. Just the two of us.

(At left, Jeffrey De Munn as Andrew; Christopher Collet as Martin)
Photo Credit: Susan Cook

ANDREW: (tense) *This will not work,* Elise.

ELISE:　　So it still hurts. Good. After all these years of silence, I wasn't sure.

ANDREW: Your silence, not mine. I kept in touch, only Martin wrote back.

ELISE:　　I wrote. I'm still waiting for an answer.

(At left Kate Nelligan as Elise; Jeffrey De Munn as Andrew)
Photo Credit: Susan Cook

MARTIN: I wanted you to be at Parent's Day. Both of you. I thought maybe if I read the essay in front of everyone, and you'd be there all fixed up, maybe he'd see what he was missing . . .

ELISE: And have us back?

MARTIN: Why not?

ELISE: You dreamer.

MARTIN: 'Cause I'd be gone all year. You'd have all that time to see each other again. He could take you dancing on the roof of that hotel in Brooklyn, just like the old days.

ELISE: The St. George? He told you about that?

MARTIN: You did.

ELISE: Never.

MARTIN: In New Mexico. At that motel. The night we left Mr. Haverstock.

ELISE: *Sid?* Is that all he was to you—Mr. Haverstock?

MARTIN: What was he to you, Mom? What were any of them?

ELISE: I believe the word is *husbands*, darling. And with any luck, fathers.

MARTIN: I only have one father.

ELISE: Is it so strange that I'd want to make a normal life for us? We came close with Sid. I almost learned to cook.

MARTIN: It's Andrew's party.

ELISE: Ah. The fog lifts.

MARTIN: I told him I was bringing a mystery date. A girl from school.

ELISE: Oh, Martin, stories and stories and stories.

MARTIN: I must be crazy. Are you real angry?

ELISE: I don't know what I am. I feel terribly betrayed.

MARTIN: Why do I have to give up on him just because you did? *(Sees that he's gone too far)* I'll call him and cancel.

ELISE: *(distant)* I think that's the best idea.

MARTIN: Okay.

ELISE: Do me up.

MARTIN: *(obeying)* I'm sorry, Mom.

ELISE: *(being fastened)* Is he bald? He was always touching his hairline.

MARTIN: Women find him attractive.

ELISE: Do they now. He's seeing someone?

MARTIN: It's nothing, she's a kid.

ELISE: Bastard . . .

MARTIN: Mom!

ELISE: What do you do together, you and your father . . . and this kid?

MARTIN: He's teaching me to fly.

ELISE: He owns an airplane?

MARTIN: Just pretend. He gives commands, I carry 'em out.

ELISE: Yes, that sounds like Andrew.

MARTIN: He's trying to start his own magazine.

ELISE: I'm sure he'll succeed.

MARTIN: I showed him your picture.

ELISE: I have to run, angel . . . what picture?

MARTIN: The gypsy one. With the cigarette.

ELISE: How could you, I look hideous.

MARTIN: He didn't think so.

ELISE: He's being polite. He was always a gentleman. To give him a little more than his due.

MARTIN: He remembers dancing in Brooklyn. The picture reminded him.

ELISE: He said that? Martin, is this another story?

MARTIN: He got all quiet when he talked about you.

ELISE: What else did he say? This is silly, you really must watch that imagination of yours, it's contagious.

MARTIN: He wants us back, I know he does. He got this new apartment right after Parent's Day, it's enormous.

ELISE: Then why hasn't he been in touch?

MARTIN: He asked the same thing about you.

ELISE: Martin, look at me! Did he mention Brooklyn? You never showed him the picture, did you? Honestly, darling, you must stop making up these stories.

MARTIN: If he saw you again, though. In the special dress, the silky one.

ELISE: Angel. You're so sure of yourself.

MARTIN: I know what he's thinking. He's my father.

ELISE: Is it a big party?

MARTIN: Pretty big.

ELISE: *(beat)* It would be quite a scene, wouldn't it. The two of us waltzing back into his life arm in arm. I wonder if any of the old gang . . .

MARTIN: Who's that?

ELISE: I used to make quite the impression when I entered a room. I stood perfectly still, and everything moved in my direction.

MARTIN: What's that smell?

ELISE: The coffee. (MARTIN *exits)* Oh, Martin, I told you to keep an eye on it, honestly, you'd forget your head if it wasn't attached to your body. Never mind, I'll grab a cup on the way to work, I'm centuries late . . .

(MARTIN *has reentered with charred, smoking coffee pot.)*

MARTIN: Right through the bottom.

ELISE: Oh, well, no use crying over burnt metal. Give me a kiss, angel, we'll meet here at five-thirty on the nose, make it a quarter of . . .

(In a rush, ELISE *collects handbag, sketch portfolio, whatever.)*

MARTIN: What's the big plan, dinner? Movies?

ELISE: On your last night in town? Doesn't that call for something more along the lines of a surprise party?

MARTIN: Really? You'll come?

ELISE: After all the pains taken, how could I disappoint? We should call and warn him, it's only fair. But on the other hand, in love and war. *(Blows kiss)* Well? (MARTIN *catches it to his lips)* What a pair we are, you and I.

(ELISE *exits.* MARTIN *stands with coffee pot smoking in hand, a smile on his face. Lights fade.)*

END OF ACT ONE

ACT
TWO

ACT TWO

EMMA'S PLACE

(Books, periodicals, newspapers, a cramped space, that of a woman who thinks little about her own needs and lives for others. Enter ELISE and EMMA in semidarkness.)

EMMA: Come in, come in . . .

ELISE: Where were you?

EMMA: Up cleaning Cedric's place.

ELISE: What would that man do without you.

(EMMA turns on lights. ELISE is dressed and made up stunningly. EMMA is dressed for cleaning. ELISE's manner is edgy, distracted, but she is attempting to master her nerves.)

EMMA: My God, Elise, you look gorgeous! Why? I mean, what are you doing here, isn't this your night with Martin?

ELISE: He's with his father. They've been seeing each other in secret.

EMMA: Oh dear, that's terrible, that's . . . sit, sit.

ELISE: *(not sitting)* The surprise party—it's Andrew's. I'm the mystery date. Emma, I'm terrified.

EMMA: You're going to see him?

ELISE: Have you anything on hand of a liquid nature? I'm in need of courage tonight, Dutch or otherwise.

EMMA: I'll make coffee . . . *(starts off)*

ELISE: Stay.

EMMA: *(beat)* It was bound to happen sooner or later. The whole gang's been talking about it all year.

ELISE: What do they say? What do *you* say?

EMMA: I think you've both been waiting to see who gives in first.

ELISE: So what's new.

EMMA: Martin, for one.

ELISE: Yes. He wants this so badly.

EMMA: And you don't?

ELISE: Who knows what I want anymore? I want the *passion.* I want that terrible closeness we all once had.

EMMA: Wasn't that mainly a housing problem?

ELISE: You know what I mean.

EMMA: We were young. No money, no jobs, what else did we have but each other?

ELISE: I ask too much, don't I? Why does everything feel so small and selfish and trivial now?

EMMA: I might have some wine. *(Starts off)*

ELISE: *(slips out flask)* Oh, look what I found. Just a glass, my dear. Never mind.

(ELISE *pours shot into cap, pops it down, pours another quickly.)*

EMMA: It's the romance you miss, not the struggle. That goes on, with or without the dreamers.

ELISE: You still believe, don't you? My darling Red Emma, the last holdout.

EMMA: It's not a religion, for God's sake—it's fact and process. You think the world will stand by forever while so few people grab so very much of it for themselves?

ELISE: They've certainly been slow to object.

EMMA: Enough, we'll only argue.

ELISE: Oh but let's, let's argue like the old days, late into the night over black coffee and cigarettes. Let's live for something bigger than rent and the price of hamburger. God, doesn't it make you sick?

EMMA: Not a bit.

ELISE: Why can't I be like you, given to an idea, to something that doesn't change.

EMMA: You mean someone who doesn't run off.

ELISE: He didn't run off.

EMMA: Fine.

ELISE: Why is it you so disliked him?

EMMA: Two reasons. Always, whatever the subject, Stalin, Hitler, architecture, the movement, always, always he had to be *right.*

ELISE: He always was.

EMMA: And that's the other reason. A man without innocence. And finally, a coward.

ELISE: No, no, never that.

EMMA: Why defend him? He took the easy way out, a uniform, a gun. Someone his age, almost thirty, and with a family. You think without the war you'd still be together? A loner is a loner.

ELISE: He might have changed.

EMMA: For you? Nonsense. You were the beauty, he was the leader—our glorious couple, in love with a moment in time—it was a house of cards, the first wind and, whhht!

ELISE: You're in a strange mood tonight.

EMMA: *(pause)* Cedric was arrested.

ELISE: What?

EMMA: They grabbed him on the el this morning, took him off somewhere for deportation.

ELISE: But why? He wasn't even a party member.

EMMA: Why, why, as if they need a reason. He gets letters from China with Mao Tse Tung on the stamp. He hates the rich. He writes books full of long words—to them, that's a Communist.

ELISE: I'm so sorry. Do you want to be alone?

EMMA: Who *wants* to be alone?

ELISE: What'll you do?

EMMA: Carry on. He's gone, but there's still the work. They ransacked his apartment. His address book has our names. Careful on the phone. You see, it didn't end with McCarthy.

ELISE: *(abstracted)* Cedric proposed to me, that summer on the commune. His father was a duke. Imagine, here but for Andrew stands a duchess. Isn't it stupid to marry for love.

EMMA: Maybe you *should* go, Elise.

ELISE: I'm sorry. That was an awful thing to say.

EMMA: What are you doing here?

ELISE: Martin left without me. I was late getting home—
with a few pit stops along the way, of course. I've been
putting on my face, and taking it off, and putting it back
on again ever since.

EMMA: You didn't answer my question.

ELISE: You're angry.

EMMA: Yes.

ELISE: What have I done?

EMMA: You came to see Lew.

ELISE: Lew? He's here?

EMMA: Don't. He told me you've met him at the Copper
Pot for drinks. Twice.

ELISE: Advice about the house. Oh, Emma, you don't
think I'd do anything so underhand.

EMMA: You don't mean to, I know.

ELISE: It's *you* I had to see. Please believe me, you're the
only one who makes me feel the least bit forgiven.

EMMA: But you take advantage. And I let you, it's my fault
—you just don't understand your power.

ELISE: Power? What power have I ever had over anything?

EMMA: Over Martin. Me. Your friends . . . even Lew. He talks about nothing else, day and night; what's she like, when did you meet her, has she mentioned me . . .

ELISE: He's such a baby . . .

EMMA: And you are wonderfully blind, Elise. It's your great strength. My God, the hours I have spent talking politics to some poor fool while he glances over my head at guess-who across the room, surrounded by admirers. You never knew, you took it for granted. After all, who am I? The Friend. The Passport-to-an-Introduction.

ELISE: I wasn't even there when you met Lew. You brought him to my place.

EMMA: Who cares about that stupid man, take him, get him away from me, he talks nonsense, I can't stand having him underfoot all the time . . . *(stifles sob)*

ELISE: It's Cedric, isn't it?

EMMA: All we did was talk. I'd go up. He'd come down. It was enough. They'll never let him back.

ELISE: *(approaches* EMMA) I'll stay . . .

EMMA: Don't touch me. I'm fragile but coping.

ELISE: *(beat)* Cedric never proposed.

EMMA: I know.

ELISE: Why do I say these things?

EMMA: He slept with you once. You struck him as shallow.

ELISE: *(surprise)* Well, he's wrong. And a terrible lover. You missed nothing.

EMMA: Thank you for telling me.

ELISE: *(offers flask)* First aid?

EMMA: *(tetchy)* Can't you wait for a glass!

(Pause. They laugh. EMMA exits to the kitchen. Alone, ELISE is suddenly agitated again, checking her face in compact mirror. LEW, having appeared quietly, watches her for a moment.)

LEW: Like what you see?

ELISE: Lewis! Good evening.

LEW: I thought you were spoken for tonight.

ELISE: I was and I am. Emma had a little upset. I thought I should drop by.

LEW: What about later?

ELISE: Later hasn't happened yet.

LEW: Is that a yes or a no? (EMMA *reenters with mug and wineglass.* LEW *covers*) I was just on my way out. Emma's been kind enough to let me use her couch . . .

EMMA: I think she already knows that, Lew.

LEW: Don't suppose either of you good ladies would care to join me?

EMMA: I'm afraid you can't stay here after tomorrow.

LEW: Getting too comfortable, huh? Time to face the music.

EMMA: I'm glad you understand.

LEW: I'll just head on down to the Copper Pot for a bite, maybe stick around till closing. *(Beat)* Careful who you talk to about that house idea, Elise. I made some calls. It smells big. Real big. I'll run it down for you . . . any time. *(Beat)* Say, what's the deal with the blue laws around here? When do they stop serving Sunday?

EMMA: We wouldn't know, Lew.

LEW: *(gets the message. Starting out, he hesitates)* Good night. *(Exits)*

EMMA: *(having poured, lifts mug)* And here we are again. To us?

ELISE: You see—I begged Andrew to take us back. I know that's why he hasn't been in touch.

EMMA: Ah. The post card.

ELISE: It was more than a post card, Emma. It was my future, spilling onto paper, scribble, scribble, scribble—

you know how I get under the influence. New Mexico somewhere. Some hotel, some bar, the drive east. Martin asleep down the hall. Always, till then, I felt my life moving forward to a better time. Then the ground slipped under my feet. Just a little. And I felt completely alone.

EMMA: Aren't we being a little dramatic?

ELISE: No, I saw what I was that night, so clearly—begging Andrew to rescue me. Or Sid. Or the others. I've always been the same, full of wonderful plans, but lacking some vital gear to set me in motion and make me sufficient, without a man. Oh God, Emma, just to stand before him whole, that's all I want. "There Andrew, I ask nothing, I need nothing, only you." Then I have to go and ruin the whole thing. *(Beat)* Dear oh dear, listen to her. You're right, I'm full of Russian blood tonight, bring on the balalaikas.

EMMA: You know, Andrew called Cedric your first month back. He wanted to know was it true you were staying down here.

ELISE: *(beat)* You tell me this *now?*

EMMA: Cedric hates meddling. He said two things in this country were inevitable without our help—the Revolution, and your reunion with Andrew.

ELISE: Dear old Cedric.

ELSEWHERE (ANDREW'S PLACE)

(Enter ANDREW *with a large cake.)*

EMMA: People don't get over you, Elise. Go to your party. Just be yourself.

ELISE: *(brighter)* Incandescent? Ravishing? Irresistible? Yes, I see what you mean. And with a young man beside me anyone would die to call their own. *(They hug)*

EMMA: Next week? Same time? Same place?

(ELISE *exits, then* EMMA *as . . .)*

(Enter PENNY *quietly, watching* ANDREW *place candles carefully in cake. The room is now furnished, but there is still some junk and boxes in corners, plus spare party supplies which define the space as a utility area not to be used by guests. Party noises from next door, and the sound of someone playing the piano very well, perhaps a piece by Jelly Roll Morton.)*

PENNY: You sweet old thing. (ANDREW *turns suddenly)* Don't worry, no one's coming in here—he's got 'em all spellbound.

ANDREW: *(animated)* Can you believe that little son of a gun? Where'd he learn to tell stories like that, non-stop for hours, my own kid . . . !

PENNY: You might want to watch him with the liquor.

ANDREW: What the hell, let him make a few mistakes of his own, he's had enough mothering for one lifetime.

PENNY: He's overboard, sweetie. He wants so much to

make a good impression. Just let him know he has nothing to prove—he's sixteen, for God's sake . . .

ANDREW: And he's twenty-five, and he's ten. At his age it's all fever and hormones. Just watch, the minute his girlfriend shows up everything'll be fine.

PENNY: Is that what the big book said?

ANDREW: Book?

PENNY: The one you've been underlining all week? *The Psychology of the Adolescent?*

ANDREW: A spy in my house, eh? What else did you learn from all those clean-living upright Calvinists back on the farm?

PENNY: Very funny.

ANDREW: He's my son, kitten. I think I know what he's going through, thank you. Hey, you've been a great sport about fitting in here, don't think I haven't noticed . . .

PENNY: Talk about unbelievable . . . !

ANDREW: *Now* what?

PENNY: You two seem to think, I don't know, like you're this fabulous father-son team, one of those portraits on the boardwalk with a hole in it where every woman in the city's just dying to stick her head and get her picture taken.

ANDREW: Is someone getting a little complicated here?

PENNY: God forbid, we can't have that.

ANDREW: Penny, stop taking the damn world on your shoulders. Your father is not here drinking himself to death. Martin is not in crisis. Everyone enjoyed meeting you. Don't look for things to fix when everything's okay.

PENNY: *(finger gun)* Pow! I'm right. Keep an eye on him.

ANDREW: Come here you little snoop. You gazelle. You sexy zoo creature, you.

(They kiss warmly. MARTIN *bursts in, flushed as* ANDREW *and* PENNY *separate fast.)*

MARTIN: Hey, Dad, that bald guy out there with the earring and the tee shirt . . .

ANDREW: Hey, out, out of here . . .

MARTIN: Isn't he on the television . . . ?

ANDREW: That's Mister Clean, now am-scray . . .

MARTIN: And who's that Chinese guy that keeps talking in a funny voice?

ANDREW: Oh, Jesus, Lee Chen must be doing his Milton Berle imitation. Just tell him "Uncle Milty, *how jee-la,*" he'll die a happy man.

MARTIN: *How jee-la?*

ANDREW: Having a good time?

MARTIN: Are you kidding? Wait'll they hear about this back at school—where's the vodka?

PENNY: Where's your date?

MARTIN: *(stops)* Date? *(Smooth)* She had a few things to take care of. Don't worry, you'll meet her.

PENNY: I was thinking more of the condition she'll find you in.

MARTIN: I can hold my liquor, Penny. Thanks for your concern.

PENNY: Don't mention it.

ANDREW: *(intervenes)* How 'bout a Moxie? We'll split one.

MARTIN: Sure.

ANDREW: *(as she goes, to* MARTIN*)* You're doing one helluva job out there. I'm starting to think this magazine thing might really take off, and no small thanks to the entertainment committee . . .

MARTIN: *(spots cake)* Hey, is that an airfield?

ANDREW: *(shy)* Zurich. The candles are landing lights. What do you think . . . I made it.

MARTIN: You? The whole thing?

ANDREW: Picked up a trick or two living solo.

MARTIN: I'll tell you my opinion, Dad. It's pretty corny.

ANDREW: *(laughs)* So it is, what the hell. Say, do you know this one *(sings)*

Oh Mister Gallagher
Yes, Mister Sheen?

(explains) Vaudeville, this is, Gallagher and Sheen, the best . . . *(sings)*

Oh Mister Gallagher
Yes, Mister Sheen?
Who was that lady that I saw you with last night?
Dum-dum-dum-de-dah-dah-dah . . . (lost)

(explains) See, Gallagher takes her out in a rowboat and they're spooning away, when this wave comes and sploosh, into the water—they swim for their life, then, this is Gallagher *(sings)*

Pulled her up upon the shore
Now she's mine forever more
Who, the lady, Mister Gallagher?
No, the rowboat, Mister Sheen!

(laughs) What a team. Father took me . . . unforgettable. He knew every record by heart. *(beat)* Well, I guess we'll leave the entertaining to you.

MARTIN: That was terrific, Dad.

ANDREW: Listen, kiddo, I had a thought. How'd you like a little company on the trip over?

MARTIN: You mean Europe?

ANDREW: Leave early, take a few weeks, Burma, Chinese border, show you some of the old army haunts, maybe shoot a travel piece, coffee–table stuff, then drop you off in Switzerland.

MARTIN: Just you and me?

ANDREW: Spend some time. Catch up.

MARTIN: Mom's never been abroad.

ANDREW: *Us*, Marty. Just the two of us.

MARTIN: You really hate her, don't you.

ANDREW: Hey, kiddo, how 'bout we stick to the subject here. I don't hate her, why should I hate her?

MARTIN: Aren't you even just a little curious to see what she's like?

ANDREW: Your mother is an all-or-nothing kind of person. Clean break, that's how she wants it, no calls, no letters —fine with me . . .

MARTIN: But if she had been in touch, just say—would you want to talk to her?

ANDREW: Sometimes things happen in your life that seem very, very important at the time, but in the long run you realize they're just not the main event. It's no use living in the past.

MARTIN: Who wants to live there? I just want someone to talk about it.

ANDREW: Hey, tell ya what, and this is a promise. We travel together, and I'll jawbone you till my teeth fall out, okay? Till then, just remember, there's two sides to every story, and whatever you may have heard—I was always ready to listen to their side of things, even to help out where I could, and they know that. They always knew. Which is why, just by the way, a certain gentleman who's called me some pretty colorful names over the years—and in print—but a damn good man all the same, when he was arrested this morning, it wasn't the others he used his one phone call to ask for advice. What we might have done, if we'd all held together.

MARTIN: *(abruptly)* Dad, was I a mistake?

ANDREW: Okay, Marty, what's going on here?

MARTIN: I want to know.

ANDREW: Who the hell ever put an idea like that in your head?

MARTIN: It's just there.

ANDREW: Cut the games. All night I've been smelling the old routines, the hints, the innuendo, slippy-sliding around, I didn't like it then, I don't like it now. Something's on your mind, you look me in the eye and spit it out.

MARTIN: All right, my date is Mom.

ANDREW: *(pause)* Elise? She's coming here? Are you crazy?

MARTIN: No, Dad, I am not crazy.

ANDREW: She put you up to it. It's okay, you can tell me, I know the way she can back people into a corner.

MARTIN: It was me. I wanted you to see each other.

ANDREW: Why?

MARTIN: Why do you think?

ANDREW: I think you're picking up some very bad ideas about what's acceptable behavior. You never pull this kind of stunt on me. That woman is a disruptive, unreliable and very treacherous individual . . .

MARTIN: Don't say that. She's generous. She's kind. Okay, maybe she's a little different, but there's no law against that. She cares, Dad. About everyone. I've seen her buy a whole meal for a total stranger just 'cause they were out on the street. People love her. Everyone does. You did, once. *(Beat)* Didn't you?

ANDREW: This isn't for now.

MARTIN: Oh, *that* one.

ANDREW: Enough. Tonight's not the end of the world.

MARTIN: Good to know, Dad.

ANDREW: *(sharp)* Hey. I mean it. No more.

MARTIN: I'm sorry. Let's have a party.

ANDREW: When they're gone, maybe—we'll see. Now let's set fire to this damn airport and haul it outside.

MARTIN: You bet.

ANDREW: When she gets here, I want *you* to answer the door. I'll go out and talk to her in the hall.

MARTIN: Don't worry, Dad, she won't show up. It's Parent's Day. Another pipe dream.

ELSEWHERE (ELISE'S PLACE)

(Enter LEW, *hopping like a frog, followed by* ELISE, *both giddy.)*

LEW: *(frog noise)* Grrrk-grrrk, turn on the full moon, I can't see my darn lily-pad.

ELISE: *(laughing)* Stop it, you goof, on your feet and behave.

ANDREW: How 'bout a hand with the candles?

LEW: *(lighting candle in* ELISE's *place)* And God said, "Let there be light."

ELISE: And Elise said, "No monkey business." I'll get the ground plans.

LEW: *(brandishing bottle)* And two straws.

ELISE: Lewis, I did not happen by the Copper Pot in search of hanky-panky. We have a house to discuss, is that understood?

LEW: You have my word as a gentleman, and a reptile.

(ELISE *exits.* ANDREW *and* MARTIN *have lit all the candles on the cake.)*

MARTIN: I'd like to travel with you, Dad. The two of us.

ANDREW: Everything's gonna work out fine, champ. Just go easy. *(Indicating cake)* That's your end.

(ANDREW *and* MARTIN *lift the cake and start out.* AN-DREW *breaks into song, and after a moment,* MARTIN *too)*

Hail, hail, the gang's all here
what the heck do we care
what the heck do we care

BOTH: *Hail, hail, the gang's all here*
What the heck do we care now . . .

(They exit. Meanwhile, LEW *lights more of* ELISE's *candles, takes a drink from his bottle for courage, readies*

himself for action by smoothing his hair, etc. Just as we
hear applause from ANDREW'*s party,* ELISE *reenters in*
robe, hair down, ground plans in hand.)

LEW: Oh, mama, the way you look.

ELISE: Beware, Lewis. There's danger in candlelight.

LEW: We'll see about that, lady.

(LEW *scoots over on the couch to make room.* ELISE *notes*
this and moves pointedly to the table, where she spreads
her plans.)

ELISE: It's only a rough ground plan. I'm no architect.

(LEW, *acknowledging the cut, has risen to join* ELISE *at the*
table.)

LEW: What's on the side here, you planning a gymna-
sium?

ELISE: Martin's room. My son.

LEW: Half the house. Kind of disproportionate, don't you
think?

ELISE: A boy needs room to grow.

LEW: He can go outdoors every now and then, can't he?

ELISE: Other things we can discuss—not this.

LEW: You don't understand what we got here. Forget
about one house, this idea is good for a whole damn

development, Futureville, whatever, fifty, maybe a hundred units, but we gotta start with a basic layout that meets the needs of your average American family.

ELISE: The average American family does not interest me. I want a home for me and my son, *finis.*

LEW: You're quite a handful, aren't you.

ELISE: Don't change the subject.

LEW: Elise, I gotta say this, I just do. See, I went A.W.O.L. in Korea—lived on a houseboat, Chinese family took me in, aunts, cousins, grandkids. I never did sort 'em all out. But they had something I never saw before, and being with them . . . I came home a stranger, 'cause I knew how little you need to be truly happy. Feeling close to someone is all. Peaceful close. Close in your heart—the way I feel with you right now.

ELISE: How young you are.

LEW: Sound crazy? My wife thought so the time I tried to tell her.

ELISE: What you saw was a gift. The truth. Hold onto it for all you're worth.

ELSEWHERE (ANDREW'S PLACE)

(Enter MARTIN, *thoughtful. He looks around.)*

LEW: Two people can hold onto something better than one.

(MARTIN *lifts phone off sideboard, trying to decide if he should call.*)

LEW: Elise?

ELISE: *(distant)* What is it, angel?

LEW: You're a million miles away.

ELISE: Less than half a city, but never mind.

LEW: I'm very smitten with you.

ELISE: *(suddenly delighted) Smitten?* Now there's a word worth bringing back, oh *yes!*

LEW: I guess I strike you as kind of basic.

ELISE: *(gently)* Go home, Lew. Stand in front of everything you love—children, wife, the what is it, Sunshine Sky over Witchita? Imagine losing it all, and without knowing what lies ahead, because who can know that? It may be desolation, regret, and a terrible aching loneliness. Do I frighten you, I hope so. Because until you can feel the loss, but still know a yearning greater than all you're letting go, you must never dare speak the magic word.

LEW: Being what?

ELISE: *(pause)* Good-bye.

LEW: *(resolute)* Where's your phone, I'll call her right now.

(MARTIN *lifts the phone receiver to dial.*)

ELISE: Face to face, or not at all.

LEW: Shoot, Elise, why all this rigamarole, you can see as well as I can what's going on here. Will you marry me?

(MARTIN *replaces receiver.*)

ELISE: Close your eyes.

LEW: How come?

ELISE: To please your bride-to-be.

LEW: All right, I'll play. *(Closes eyes)*

ELISE: Tell me the color of my eyes.

LEW: Brown. Sort of hazel-to-brown.

ELISE: Gray-blue. And my wraparound?

LEW: That I can tell you. Green.

ELISE: And you'd have been right one night last week when it was, but tonight, alas, the accent is on rose. Pink I'd accept, but green? No, Lewis, a clear strike two.

LEW: This is silly.

ELISE: Haven't you noticed, I'm a silly woman, and I'll be your silly wife if you get this one right, which should be easy, after the intense scrutiny you've given it all evening. Am I or am I not wearing a brassiere?

LEW: Was I that obvious?

ELISE: It was sunshine to a flower. Well?

LEW: No brassiere.

ELISE: Dear man. If only the laws of gravity were so kind. Strike three. You seem to have a different woman in mind. I'm jealous.

(LEW *kisses* ELISE *suddenly. She allows it, and returns the kiss passionately.*)

LEW: I'll take you away from all this, as God is my witness.

ELISE: After so many frogs, a prince at last.

(They kiss passionately once again.)

LEW: It's a damn crime someone like you living this way, electric off, no room to breathe, garbage on the stairs. I want to help you out of here.

ELISE: *(draws away, suddenly cold)* I don't remember asking for your help.

LEW: Don't pull away. What's wrong with a little help? Like with the house.

ELISE: You're hardly in a position to be judging my life.

LEW: Take it easy. You deserve better is all. I'd like to give you what I think you're worth.

ELISE: All the right words from all the wrong men.

LEW: Look at me.

ELISE: You'll have to leave now. This was a mistake. Please forgive me, I'm expected elsewhere.

LEW: *(outburst)* Listen up, lady. I'm not letting anyone kick me out on my ass after I put in this kind of time. I had a sweet number working when you came into the Copper Pot and I dropped her *like that*, now you owe me.

ELISE: *(folds away sketch)* From prince to beast in the blink of an eye—this fairy tale is going backwards.

LEW: Look, I didn't mean that—you got me all tied up in knots.

ELISE: Please don't be here when I return. Good night, Lew.

LEW: You're going out like that?

ELISE: But this is me, unadorned. Why do I feel so horribly sober. *(Exits)*

(As LEW collects himself and exits slowly, nonplussed, PENNY enters to MARTIN.)

PENNY: So there you are.

MARTIN: Is it over?

PENNY: Some crowd, huh? A little on the ritzy side for us in the business of hippo turds. How 'bout a smile, I could use it . . .

MARTIN: I'm leaving now.

PENNY: Hey, I know what it's like being stood up. There's other girls, summer hotel, cute guy like you.

MARTIN: Through the service door. I'll catch an early train in the morning. I'm never going to see my parents again.

PENNY: Are you drunk?

MARTIN: No, Penny. My *mother* is drunk. She's at a bar somewhere. Or maybe at home. Maybe with a man, who knows? I started to call her, but what's the point, she'd just make up some story to protect me. And I'd pretend to believe it to protect her. It's a little game we play called "No Secrets." You weren't supposed to be here tonight. And she was.

PENNY: *(beat)* I see.

MARTIN: Do you? I was beginning to think no one saw anything, ever. Except Andrew. Because he never lets the little stuff get in the way. You look at what's in front of you and you call it by its name. I want to sleep with you.

PENNY: *(beat)* Sure. Can you wait'll I get my purse?

MARTIN: You think I'm joking?

PENNY: Martin, what's going on?

MARTIN: We've been flirting all night, that's what. No, no, let's get this exactly right—we've been flirting right from the start. Animals going wild. Stiff bristle?

PENNY: I was not flirting with you.

MARTIN: Will you come with me, yes or no?

PENNY: Of course not, are you crazy?

MARTIN: Very good. A clear, simple answer—no evasions, no mysteries. Thank you, Penny. Good night.

PENNY: Would you please stop being like this.

MARTIN: What, honest?

PENNY: Creepy. Just shut up and sit down for a minute.

MARTIN: You knew I was back here. You followed me. Why? To see how I was doing, okay, that's the excuse, that's the *game,* but the reason, Penny? The real reason. You see what I mean.

PENNY: You don't have to impress me, Martin.

MARTIN: I'm sick of the bullshit. I'm sick of pretending I don't see what's going on. Just say it, for God's sake, why is that so difficult, you've been flirting with me, *say it, say it!*

PENNY: No, Martin. *(Beat)* Yes. A little. Maybe. Look, I've noticed the glances. All right, I've *enjoyed* them. The smiles. Yes, the danger even—wondering if Andrew noticed. I've never been coveted by two generations of the same family.

MARTIN: You see? Underneath, everything's so simple. You want me. I want you. Sniff sniff.

PENNY: Would you cut it out, your father's right outside!

MARTIN: *(loud, towards door)* I know where my father is! This has nothing to do with him.

PENNY: You are a naughty little boy.

MARTIN: And you are so damn beautiful.

PENNY: What an operator. I'm starting to see your technique, Mister Martin. A little mystery, a shock attack, I drop my guard and zip, in for the kill.

MARTIN: *(puts hand on her breast)* This feels so right.

PENNY: Take your hand away.

MARTIN: Tonight is for us.

PENNY: The hand.

MARTIN: Are you afraid of my father?

PENNY: *(removes hand)* That's enough. I won't breathe a

word about this, but you have to behave now . . . talk about outrageous.

MARTIN: *(suddenly defenseless)* Hold me. Please. I won't try anything. I need someone close to me.

PENNY: Oh, Martin, Martin, Martin, what are we going to do with you?

(PENNY *holds him comfortingly. Unseen by* PENNY, AN-DREW *enters from party.* MARTIN *sees him and responds by taking* PENNY's *hand, kissing it, then brushes his lips up her arm as she starts to yield.)*

ANDREW: Penny, go inside.

PENNY: *(breaking away suddenly)* Poops. Thank God. You better find out what's going on here. I think your son's in big trouble.

ANDREW: *(controlled fury)* Inside. Now. *(As* PENNY*exits)* All right, Martin, let's have it, and this better the hell be damned good.

MARTIN: Want to split a Moxie? Or should we just look each other in the eye and spit it out.

ANDREW: What are you trying to prove?

MARTIN: I don't know. And I don't even care.

ANDREW: *(beat)* Her. This is all *her.*

MARTIN: It's me, Dad, I'm back. I'm back.

(Pause. Enter PENNY, *hesitant, looking nervously over her shoulder.)*

PENNY: Andrew, someone just arrived, she asked for you, I don't know what to tell her . . .

*(*ELISE *enters in her wraparound. All look at her.)*

ELISE: Hello, everyone. Sorry I'm late.

ANDREW: Elise!

MARTIN: Mom, what are you doing here?

ELISE: I believe I was invited.

MARTIN: But like that. You came here like that?

ANDREW: I'll handle this. Martin, Penny, wait outside.

ELISE: No need, Andrew, I come in peace.

ANDREW: I can imagine. A little earlier and you could have disrupted the entire evening. I hope you're not too disappointed.

ELISE: I'll get over it. And who might this be?

PENNY: My name is Penny.

ELISE: Penny! You didn't used to settle for such small change.

MARTIN: Mom . . .

ELISE: What, dear?

MARTIN: Just . . . behave, okay?

ELISE: *(sweetly smiling)* She's very attractive, and I admire her shoes. Hello, Penny, I'm the former Mrs. Andrew, and this is our son. Oh, that's right, you've met. Welcome to our—what shall we call it?—reunion.

PENNY: Excuse me. *(Exits)*

ELISE: Not much fight in that one.

ANDREW: You've made your grand entrance, you've stirred up trouble, now what?

ELISE: Nothing. I've exhausted my repertoire.

ANDREW: That'll be the day.

MARTIN: Don't argue, please.

ELISE: Friendly banter, darling. No, no, when Andrew and I go for blood—what did they used to say?—after us the Revolution would be an anticlimax. Your father was not amused. About himself he has, how much humor would you say, Andrew, on a scale of one to zero?

ANDREW: You haven't changed.

ELISE: Why thank you, you've held up pretty well yourself.

ANDREW: That's not what I meant . . . oh.

ELISE: Am I going too fast? You could keep up, once.

(Both ANDREW *and* ELISE *are trying desperately to master their feelings, but both are shaken by the sight of each other, and by the sudden total return of old emotional habits they had perhaps allowed themselves to believe long dead.)*

ANDREW: Still showing off? For who, Elise? Those days are gone, there's no one left to impress.

ELISE: Was it for them? Is that what we've decided? *(Beat)* Oh, Andrew, let's bury the hatchet. Hasn't our little war of silence outlived whatever use it never served?

ANDREW: I'll say good-bye to my guests, then we can sit down together and have a quiet talk. Is that agreeable?

ELISE: The imperious command followed by the rhetorical question—vintage Andrew!

ANDREW: Fine. You tell me what *you'd* like to do.

ELISE: It's a profoundly sane and rational plan.

ANDREW: May we consider it settled?

MARTIN: She's just teasing. It doesn't mean anything.

ELISE: Thank you, dear.

ANDREW: I know what she's doing, I know exactly.

ELISE: Yes, you always know, don't you. Tell us how to make the perfect martini, and the correct way to say Carib*be*an, or is it Ca*rí*bbean—and how to address the factory workers so they'll feel unity with us their creative comrades . . .

ANDREW: Are you trying to provoke me?

ELISE: Oh, phooey, Andrew, can't you take a little good–natured ribbing.

MARTIN: She just says stuff, Dad, ignore it. Talk to her.

ELISE: Wisdom from babes. Talk to me.

ANDREW: *(measured)* We should come to some formal arrangement about Martin—his schooling and so on. I'd like to contribute.

ELISE: To take charge, you mean. To send him where he'll learn dates and names and how to play the game. You certainly have changed sides.

ANDREW: Same old moves—one foot on politics, the other on sentiment, and shift weight to keep us all off balance.

ELISE: Damn it, Andrew, you're the one that provokes, you and your Olympian calm. It's an act, look, look at your fists all clenched up in your pocket. Take them out, show Martin the beast. God knows he's seen my faults.

ANDREW: *(tense) This will not work, Elise.*

ELISE: So it still hurts. Good. After all these years of silence, I wasn't sure.

ANDREW: Your silence, not mine. I kept in touch, only Martin wrote back.

ELISE: I wrote. I'm still waiting for an answer.

ANDREW: Don't do this, *please*. Always it starts with a small lie and ends in some bottomless fiction.

ELISE: You didn't get my letter? Andrew, is this cruelty, or extreme tact?

(Pause. Both ANDREW *and* ELISE *are genuinely puzzled.)*

MARTIN: *(blurts)* Shouldn't we say good-bye to the guests? Wasn't that the plan? Then we won't be disturbed, okay? I'll do it, I'll take care of everything . . .

ELISE: Let Andrew. A break might jog his memory.

MARTIN: Mom, would you get off the letter, forget about it, just talk, have a drink . . . I'll be back in a minute.

ELISE: What's going on?

MARTIN: *(starting out)* Nothing.

ELISE: Martin, look at me.

MARTIN: *(trying to shrug it off)* It got lost in the mail, you put the wrong address, who cares about a stupid letter, you're together now, that's what you wanted, that's what you wrote . . . *(stops suddenly, caught)*

ELISE: I see. And did you simply snoop, or did you snoop and destroy.

ANDREW: Martin, was there a letter?

MARTIN: *(to* ELISE) You don't want him to see it.

ELISE: Did you keep my letter? Martin, answer me.

MARTIN: *(confused)* You never show up. We make all these plans. I didn't know if you'd be here tonight . . .

ELISE: In which case, what? You'd show your father the damning evidence and I'd stand exposed . . . ?

MARTIN: But I didn't. You're here.

ELISE: This wasn't worthy of you, Martin.

(MARTIN, *in frustration, takes the letter from his jacket pocket and throws it on the floor.)*

ANDREW: Put that away.

ELISE: No. What's done is done. Martin . . . ?

MARTIN: *(urgent)* Mom . . . you don't remember what you wrote, you don't remember anything from that night.

ELISE: *(steely)* My forgiveness has limits. (MARTIN *picks*

up and hands her the letter. She extends it to ANDREW)
For you.

ANDREW: Are you sure?

ELISE: Thank you. Yes.

ANDREW: *(opens it and pulls out jumbled cocktail nap-kins)* What's all this?

ELISE: Cocktail napkins. The Campfire Lounge, if mem-ory serves. Not my finest hour.

MARTIN: It was just that one night. She hardly ever drinks. Mom, take it back, please . . .

ELISE: *(to* ANDREW) Shall I tell you what it says? I missed you. Not a day went by I didn't regret having left. But, you see, *you* left *me* once—true, with the war for an alibi and, true, you came back . . . that time. But what if you'd left me again one day, as it seemed all too clear you would—and so, very stupidly, I acted first . . .

MARTIN: Mom, that's not what you wrote . . .

ELISE: Let's say it was. And let's say you did not sneak it off the bureau that night knowing I was confused, be-cause I taught you never to abuse anyone in their dark hour. And when the letter arrived, and your father learned how I felt, what was his reply? Tell me, An-drew?

ANDREW: *(shaken)* Elise. A little restraint. A little bal-ance. That's all I ever asked.

ELISE: Then why fall in love with me?

ANDREW: And if you wanted all this passionate excess . . .

ELISE: Yes. Mysteries.

ANDREW: Water under the bridge.

ELISE: Is it?

(ELISE *takes out a cigarette, testing a memory.* ANDREW *understands. With a practiced gesture, he slips an expensive lighter from his pocket, lights her cigarette. She notes the lighter.*)

It used to be wooden matches. You've come up in the world. And I'll bet you still don't smoke.

ANDREW: *(softer)* I would like to help out in some way—financially, whatever.

ELISE: No doors are shut.

ANDREW: Maybe . . . at the end of the summer . . . before Martin leaves, we could plan a weekend.

MARTIN: You'll see us?

ELISE: Shhh, darling, you've meddled enough.

ANDREW: Do you still—ever dance?

ELISE: They closed the Saint George.

ANDREW: Yes. Remember the commune?

ELISE: Who could forget. Monday–night folk dancing . . .

ANDREW: God, yes, in the barn. Cedric, Emma, Phillip, all the true believers out there trying to learn, what was it?

ELISE: The Wedding Stomp . . .

BOTH: *(shared joke)* . . . of the Ukrainian Goatherd.

ELISE: *(laughs)* With whom we'd all, come the Revolution, be tending our flocks one day . . .

ANDREW: . . . in Central Park, no doubt. *(Animated, to* MARTIN) Lise and I . . . *(corrects himself)* Your mother and I had our own secret victrola, no one knew. We'd sneak away from the barn with an armful of 78s . . .

ELISE: And that horrible cheap vodka . . .

ANDREW: You could drink any Russian we ever met straight under the table . . .

ELISE: You see, darling, a thing of legend, my capacity . . .

ANDREW: Take turns winding that infernal machine . . .

ELISE: . . . and dancing, dancing in the woods all alone to, oh God, Rudy Vallee . . .

ANDREW: Eddy Duchin . . .

ELISE: Horror, so bourgeois, Guy Lombardo, our dirty little vice . . .

ANDREW: Imagine if they'd caught us!

ELISE: The Goatherds!

ANDREW: The Holy Warriors!

ELISE: *(to* MARTIN) With me, your father could relax and be silly, oh so silly, and human, and adorable *(sings)*

*I saw you last night and got
that old feeling*

(She sings next line and hums rest of verse. ELISE *moves towards* ANDREW, *humming as the old movements fill her body. For a moment,* ANDREW *resists what he's feeling, but finally begins to yield.* PENNY *enters, trying to control her fury.)*

PENNY: You know, I think it would be a terrifically good idea to have at least one person saying good-bye out there who actually belongs to this family.

MARTIN: *(pushing her out of room)* Leave us alone. Close the door. No one comes in here.

ANDREW: He overdid the drink tonight, my fault, Elise, sorry.

MARTIN: *(returns)* You're getting along now, don't stop. Keep talking.

ANDREW: Hey, champ, a little cold water on the face, eh?

MARTIN: Dance with her. *(Pulls* ELISE *towards* ANDREW *by the hand)* You two dance together, I'll go inside, I'll clean up, I'll take care of everything, you stay here alone and dance . . .

ANDREW: For Christ sake, get a hold of yourself.

MARTIN: Forget about me, I'm not here.

ANDREW: That's enough, Martin, no more!

ELISE: Don't you dare talk to him that way.

MARTIN: He's right, Mom, I had too much to drink, it's my fault.

ELISE: No one here is at fault, angel.

MARTIN: *(icy)* I ruin everything. Don't look at me. Don't make me be here.

ANDREW: Will you stop this pathetic whining? Wait in the living room.

ELISE: You have no right to order my son around. I want you to apologize.

ANDREW: He's getting away with murder, and you encourage it, all your weaknesses—the lies, the evasions, the self-pity . . .

ELISE: You bastard, I've tried to be fair, God knows I've said nothing against you in all these years, but he'll hear the truth now, all of it . . .

ANDREW: Truth? You don't know the meaning of the word. You told him I thought he was a mistake, isn't that what you said?

ELISE: Your behavior is all he needs to know that.

ANDREW: Listen to the way you bend and twist everything . . .

ELISE: Like the money?

ANDREW: Oh, yes, I can imagine what a meal you've made of *that* one . . .

MARTIN: What money . . . ?

ELISE: You see, I never even mentioned it, you have an unbiased ear, go on, Andrew, tell your son about the money . . .

ANDREW: Seeing you now, I don't regret it . . .

ELISE: Hundreds, was it? Thousands . . . ?

ANDREW: . . . is that the issue . . . ?

ELISE: . . . he never said—winnings from a poker game on the troop ship home, and how did he spend it . . .

ANDREW: . . . after three and a half years of my life . . .

ELISE: . . . on his son, on his family; *no.* On school to study architecture the way he'd talked about so passionately for years; *no . . .* !

ANDREW: . . . what was left when I returned . . . ?

ELISE: . . . he spent it on *clothes!* That's right, this man of the people, who claimed to care nothing about dress in all his life went and ordered an entire wardrobe, tailor made, just to walk among his former comrades and look as if he hadn't fallen behind.

ANDREW: That is a complete crock of shit and you know it . . .

ELISE: Ah, so we've hit a nerve at last . . .

ANDREW: I came home to nothing at all, *that's* what happened . . . !

ELISE: You never came home, only half of you, and that half was all rage and judgment . . .

ANDREW: Was I supposed to forgive what happened while I was gone . . . ?

ELISE: Nothing *happened,* Andrew . . .

ANDREW: How damn right you are, worse than nothing—

all we'd worked for, all we'd begun to build, they just walked away from it the same as they walked away from a filthy, thankless war we all agreed had to be fought, but no, once again, who did the dirty work? The same fool who organized meetings and settled disputes and trusted when he left they'd keep faith with the movement in some real way, not Cedric in his ivory tower of books and theory; in the streets, in the factory, anything, anything but abandon it to chase after their own precious careers. Well, I can play that game, too. I can out-abandon and out-career and out-dress that whole crowd till they see just how ugly their betrayal truly looks . . .

ELISE: You see every betrayal but your own.

ANDREW: I see what they let themselves forget.

ELISE: Have you forgotten the night you trembled in my arms and cried?

ANDREW: My God, now it's arms, crying . . . can't we please stick to the subject for five minutes . . . ?

ELISE: The night you showed me everything . . .

ANDREW: Fine, I was shipping out, you feel emotional, what are you trying to make it into . . .

ELISE: What you know it was . . .

ANDREW: A few tears . . .

ELISE: We touched that night. Say you don't remember it,

you who can't lie, say you don't know it was a vow to live always by the moments that bind us, to measure ourselves against the power of our hearts, and with that strength everything we dreamed of making happen was possible. Say it.

ANDREW: *(beat)* Then why did you abandon me? Why? Why, Elise?

ELISE: You're the one who went away.

ANDREW: But I returned, and you'd gone to them. I saw it the moment I stepped off the ship—you couldn't even bring yourself to look me in the eye . . .

ELISE: You fool, I was crying . . .

ANDREW: All year? Were you crying when they'd visit and the room fell stony silent when I'd dare remember that our gatherings used to have a real purpose, and you'd float off to the kitchen in, what, embarrassment at my naive persistence? And when you'd sleep alone on the couch, or stay out late with Martin—God knows where—keeping me away from all I had left to hold onto, were you crying then . . . ?

ELISE: I was afraid, Andrew—afraid of how I'd missed you —of needing you again as much as when you went away. It was pride, both of us, don't you see, stupid, foolish pride. We're human. We make mistakes. Can't we forgive now?

ANDREW: Wonderful, now we forgive. Does anything stay put with you? No wonder I had to get away. What do you want from me, what? Do you even know? Unity, Brotherhood, Power of our Hearts, it's all talk . . . and I was dumb enough to believe it meant something, for five of the most wonderful fucking years of my life I trusted . . . no more. They're through with me, I'm through with them. I'll live my own way, I'll count on no one, and I'll wear any damn thing I please . . . *(stops, shaken)*

ELISE: *(pause)* Come to me, sweet love. Tell me how you felt cheated of all that lonely, heroic time lost, and angry that things change, and we'll hold each other like we did that night until it all goes away.

ANDREW: *(pause)* No more, Elise. Between us, the silence is a better idea.

ELISE: And that, dear Andrew, is what finally makes you small . . .

ANDREW: Don't do this . . .

ELISE: . . . and sad . . .

ANDREW: I'm warning you . . .

ELISE: . . . and so very, very alone.

ANDREW: *(threatening gesture)* Shut up, shut up, damn it.

ELISE: Are you going to hit me?

ANDREW: *(murderously)* You are such a dangerous woman.

ELISE: And you're not worthy of me.

MARTIN: Mom, stop it.

ELISE: Go ahead, strike. Sooner or later you would have. Kill what comes too close.

ANDREW: *(to* MARTIN) Wait outside.

ELISE: We're going. You have what you always wanted, the goodies of the world. And the little changeling boy is mine. Come, angel, I think you've seen your father now.

MARTIN: I'm staying here.

ELISE: Get your jacket.

MARTIN: I've made up my mind. There will be no discussion.

ELISE: *(pause) Say something to him, for God's sake! Andrew!*

(Pause. ELISE *exits. Pause.)*

MARTIN: Dad?

ANDREW: *(shaken)* Fine. I'm fine. Lost my bearings for a minute. Sorry you had to see that.

MARTIN: Everything's kind of screwy tonight. She makes you all tangled up. I know why you had to get away.

ANDREW: I could use a drink. *(Beat)* No. Had enough.

MARTIN: It won't change our plans, will it? We'll still travel together . . .

PENNY: *(enters)* Everyone's gone now, and P.S., I'm real pissed off.

ANDREW: Put some coffee on, toots, we'll be right in.

PENNY: Good-bye, Andrew. Don't bother to call. *(Exits)*

ANDREW: *(beat)* She turned heads, that woman. Everywhere she went . . .

MARTIN: Penny's leaving, shouldn't you talk to her . . .

ANDREW: Everyone wanted her. Thought I never stood a chance in hell. One night, knock-knock-knock; *her.* "We must visit Russia together and see what's really going on there." She never mentioned the subject again.

MARTIN: Can I help you straighten up?

ANDREW: Hmmm? No need—cleaning lady. *(Beat)* She had such promise.

MARTIN: Dad, are we still on for Europe?

ANDREW: Something about being tied down. It's not in me. Sorry, kiddo.

MARTIN: The hotel has to know if I'm going to quit early.

ANDREW: I know what you want. It's too late for all that to happen now. We can be friends. Play it by ear. I'm glad as hell you're back.

MARTIN: I want to travel with you, Dad. I want to stay here. I don't want to see her again—ever.

ANDREW: She needs someone. Go home. Apologize. Try to work it out.

MARTIN: Why should I want to be with her when you didn't.

ANDREW: Not the point. You make a mess, you clean up.

MARTIN: Well guess what, Dad. Fuck you. Just go fuck yourself, because it's not my mess, and I'm not cleaning up after you any more . . . *(exits)*

ANDREW: Martin . . . Martin, God damn it, you're a man now, stop asking for help . . .

ELSEWHERE (ELISE'S PLACE)

(ELISE lies sprawled on fold-out bed, cover thrown aside, in a light, restless sleep. MARTIN appears in doorway holding suitcase. He watches her for a moment, turns to go, then sets down valise, enters room and tries to pull covers gently over her. A flask falls on the floor with a clatter, waking ELISE. She props herself up, groggy with booze and sleep. They look at each other.)

ELISE: So, the prodigal son returns.

MARTIN: I'm leaving.

ELISE: Yes, sneaking off into the night. Like father, like son.

MARTIN: I'm sure you'll find plenty of company at the Copper Pot.

ELISE: What did you say?

MARTIN: Isn't that how you work overtime? Isn't that what you were doing on Parent's Day?

ELISE: How dare you, after how you behaved tonight. Humiliate me in front of that man, steal my secrets, treat me like a foolish, irresponsible mother—you do not side against your own flesh and blood.

MARTIN: He's my flesh and blood, too . . .

ELISE: He is no part of my child—he ran away.

MARTIN: So did you.

ELISE: From a man who didn't want us!

MARTIN: Who'd ever want us, Mom? Look at how we are, I'm the same as you, full of the same crooked stuff inside, the same stupid pipe dreams that'll never happen . . .

ELISE: That is unworthy of you . . .

MARTIN: *(withering sarcasm)* Oh, I'm sorry, Mom, let's

play I'm the Genius Boy, and next week you'll stop drinking and get back to your poetry and Andrew will call up . . . no, let's play we don't even need him because we're going to have a home of our very own . . .

ELISE: But we are, I've promised you . . .

MARTIN: Cut it out, Mom, you know it's just a pipe dream!

ELISE: Is that so? Then suppose you tell me what you call this, Mr. Cynical, Mr. Ingratitude, Mr. Holier-Than-Thou . . . *(she rummages in bedclothes)*

MARTIN: What are you doing?

ELISE: Our land . . . ! *(Searches desperately)* . . . It was right under . . . two acres . . .

MARTIN: Put some clothes on, for God's sake.

ELISE: *(finds envelope) Voila!* Now what do you have to say for yourself?

MARTIN: *(seeing her)* You're disgusting, Mom. You're sloppy, and careless, and drunk. This is why you don't want me at home, isn't it?

ELISE: *(lowers envelope, defenseless)* Yes. It's enough I have to see myself each day—why should you have to.

MARTIN: But I *know* all this. I've always known. We have no secrets—no real ones.

(ELISE *looks away, silent.)*

MARTIN: *(takes her robe)* Put this on.

(ELISE *is motionless.)*

MARTIN: I could stay for the summer. *(Beat)* I'll find a job in the city. Sleep in the other room. I can make you happy, Mom, I know I can.

ELISE: No! It's time for you to go—to the summer, to Europe, to all the rest of it. Only promise me this: You'll never run from life, no matter how it hurts and burns . . . let it touch you everywhere, and *live!*

(Pause. MARTIN, *impossibly drawn to comfort her, to make her happy, to move past the skin that separates them, embraces her. They hold each other and fall back on the bed together, faces inches apart, he above. A dangerous moment before an irrevocable act.* ELISE *suddenly pushes him aside, and he moves away to the table, not able to look at her. Pause.)*

MARTIN: Why can't things be different?

ELISE: *(beat)* Because, my angel, none of us can choose the way we love. Any complaints, see the man in the moon.

MARTIN: *(pause)* I'd better get started.

ELISE: Oh, dear, yes, it's getting light. I used to love Monday. Shall I take a half day off? We could grab a Sloppy Joe breakfast together and talk of cabbages and kings. We'll count the stairs going down, odd ones for me, even for you.

MARTIN: No, Mom. I can wait a minute if you want to come down with me.

ELISE: You run along. I have a few things to do before I'm ready to greet the day. Take a taxi, here . . . *(reaches for her handbag)*

MARTIN: We can't afford a taxi. I'll take the bus.

ELISE: You have his eyes, you know.

MARTIN: I have my own eyes. *(Looks at bed)*

ELISE: I'll straighten all this later.

MARTIN: Sure, Mom. Sure you will. *(They hug awkwardly)* See you.

(MARTIN *exits.* ELISE *listens to the door close.)*

ELISE: May you be loved one day even half as well as I've loved you. Good-bye, my angel. *(Beat)* Good-bye.

(ELISE *sits alone. Lights fade.)*

THE END